terror
in
Quebec

Case studies of the FLQ

Gustave Morf

CLARKE, IRWIN & COMPANY LIMITED/TORONTO, VANCOUVER

© 1970 by Clarke, Irwin & Company
Limited
ISBN 0-7720-04919

A French-language edition of portions of
this book was published in Montreal by
Les Editions de l'homme in January, 1970
under the title *Le terrorisme québécois*

PRINTED IN CANADA

Contents

To my wife
Ida

Preface

In October 1970, Canada suddenly became the focus of world attention. On every continent, people were stunned by what had happened in Montreal. They asked: How could a handful of extremists become such a menace to a Western democracy? Would a united country face the threat? How would the leaders of Canada face up to the crisis?

Then came the questions: How did such a situation arise? What made the people go over the brink of discontent into insurrection? What sort of people were these terrorists?

It was in answer to these questions that the present book was written. Though it was practically finished before October 1970, not much had to be changed, apart from including the events of the current crisis — the climax of a terrorist movement which, like any war, was bound to become more and more cruel with time.

The roots of the present unrest go deep into Canada's past. The Conquest, Louis Riel and other dramatic events of French Canada's adolescence have contributed to form the French-Canadian mentality. It took a long time for English Canada to admit this and recognize that Quebec has a right — even an obligation — to keep and develop its French heritage, and that its different culture enriches the whole country.

But if Quebec has a population more imaginative, often more

passionate, and on the whole more artistically gifted than the other provinces, it also has a greater share of political ferment and turbulence. There are more violent political demonstrations and more labour conflicts in Quebec than elsewhere in Canada, and every confrontation tends to lead to greater bitterness, stronger violence and greater division than elsewhere. Moreover, French Canada is intensely afraid of being submerged by the English-speaking way of life — a way of life which, they feel, is superior to theirs only in influence. Under these circumstances it is not unnatural that Quebec has proved to be a hotbed for revolutionary ideas of every kind. This, of course, does not justify terrorist methods.

Yet the specific romantic-criminal terrorism of the FLQ would have burnt itself out long ago if it were not for the fact that its militants operated — and still operate — in a highly emotional, demanding and rebellious adolescent culture, and in a self-indulgent, permissive society which produces a rapidly increasing number of people who refuse to grow up and who believe in taking the law into their own hands.

G.M.

Montreal, Quebec
10 November, 1970

The First Wave

Bombs and Manifestos

In the spring of 1963, the province of Quebec became the stage for political acts of violence. From March to the end of May of that year a series of terrorist acts, attributed to a mysterious underground organization which called itself "Front de libération québecois" (FLQ), took place, mostly in Montreal. This wave of violence ended with the arrest of fifteen young people during the first days of June.

Since August 1917, when the home of the owner of *The Montreal Star* was dynamited by people who wanted to protest against conscription, there had been no acts of terrorism in Quebec. What had happened to bring on this outbreak?

The roots of the trouble went back to November 1962 and had to do with Mr. Donald Gordon, President of the federally owned Canadian National Railways. On a question put to him by a Créditiste Member of Parliament, Mr. Gilles Grégoire, Mr. Gordon gave an answer which inflamed the French Canadians. Mr. Grégoire had asked why, out of the company's twenty-eight top directors, only one was a French Canadian. To this Mr. Gordon had answered that promotion depended on merit, not on language, and that there were just not enough qualified French Canadians available for such a post.

Mr. Gordon worked and lived in an English atmosphere out of touch with the French-speaking population. He spoke in good faith but he did not realize that a statement which might have been accepted ten years earlier was, in 1962, no longer acceptable to the French-speaking intellectuals of Quebec. They were incensed not only by the fact that it was hard for a French Canadian to reach the top echelon of the CNR, but also by the well-known policy of English-Canadian firms not to give any promotion to French-speaking per-sonnel unless they mastered English completely. An English-speaking executive did not have to know French at all whereas a French Canadian had to know English extremely well in order to be even considered for any promotion to a higher administrative position. Even then, he was often passed by. And this in a town with a French-speaking majority!

Many French-Canadian intellectuals took the apparently cool and objective statement of Mr. Donald Gordon as a smack in the face and reacted accordingly. There was a riot in front of the head-quarters of the CNR, during which Mr. Gordon was burnt in effigy and the Union Jack was lowered and destroyed.

It is undeniable that Mr. Gordon triggered a situation which was more explosive than he had realized. Despite all his subsequent efforts to smooth things over, Quebec would never be the same. One month later, in December 1962, Dr. Marcel Chaput founded his Parti républicain du Québec, the first separatist party.

Even before that, and quite independently, a clandestine Revolutionary Committee had been formed in Montreal with the aim of achieving Quebec independence by force. A month or two later, this Committee changed its name to Réseau de résistance — Resistance Network (RR) — a designation borrowed from the Resistance fighters in France and Belgium during World War II. In the spring of 1963 approximately half of the RR broke away and renamed itself the Front de libération québecois or FLQ. It was to be a revolutionary force ready for action.

The first actions of the FLQ were quite harmless and may be interpreted as experiments aimed at testing the reactions of the public and the police. On 23 February, 1963, a bomb was placed near the CBC TV sender antenna on Mount Royal, and a second one near the private radio station CKGM. The latter was an English station which had frequently come out against separatism. Moreover, the station had ignored "warnings" by the newly born FLQ to stop playing "God save the Queen." The bomb was meant as a reminder. However, both bombs were badly constructed and failed to go off.

The failure incited the terrorist group to pay more attention to the proper fabrication of bombs. It was decided that Gabriel Hudon,

21, should be the technician entrusted with this work. From then on, the bombs were to be more reliable.

The wave of violence really began in the night of 8 March, 1963. Molotov cocktails were thrown through the windows of three different armouries in Montreal. The acts were committed by a group of three people, one watching, one throwing the bottle, the third painting the letters FLQ on the wall. These Molotov cocktails were harmless; they were filled with heating oil, a fuel that only ignites at high temperature, and they could not possibly catch fire, still less explode. The terrorists were well aware of this. They wanted the three cocktails to serve only as symbols, as a warning, not to create destruction.

The three "attacks" generated enormous publicity, which was exactly what the clandestine group wanted. They considered these attacks on three buildings of the "occupation army" as a success.

On 29 March, 1963, the Quebec monument to Wolfe, the English general who conquered the city in 1759, was toppled by unknown people. Georges Caron, speaking for the Parti républicain du Québec, declared that the act had been committed by extremists who were exasperated because of the lack of attention the independence movement was receiving from the French-language press. (Other acts of vandalism had already been committed on various monuments in the same park, without having attracted special attention.)

On 1 April, 1963, a bomb exploded on the Canadian National Railway tracks near Lemieux, Quebec, some hours before Prime Minister Diefenbaker's election campaign train was due to pass. The rail was repaired in time and the train went through without further incidents. On a nearby barn, the letters FLQ had been painted.

During the night of 2 April a time bomb was placed in front of the building of the Canadian Legion in St. Jean, Quebec. It exploded in the early morning. To their friends the FLQ explained their deed as follows:

In the night of Thursday 2 April, a suicide commando of the FLQ attacked with success the Canadian Legion, symbol of a federal institution aiming at the assimilation and the elimination of all national patriotism in Quebec. The Canadian Legion, as a servile branch of the British Imperial Legion, invariably takes a position favouring Anglo-Saxon imperialism and the exploitation which crushes our nation. The fact alone that they favour the Union Jack as the official emblem of Canada demonstrates the mentality of these infamous traitors.

At about the same time, a bomb was discovered in a corridor leading from the Central Station in Montreal to Dorchester Boulevard. It was dismantled. Another bomb exploded in the building of National Revenue on Dorchester, and on 19 April a third bomb exploded at the rear of the RCMP headquarters in Westmount, shattering windows.

In Quebec City, the letters FLQ appeared on the front door of the Lieutenant-Governor's residence and elsewhere on the walls the words "Québec libre" were written.

On 16 April, the terrorist group made an attempt at publicizing its aims by addressing the following mimeographed message to "the French Nation of Quebec":

NOTICE TO THE POPULATION OF THE STATE OF QUEBEC:

The National Liberation Front (FLQ) is a revolutionary movement consisting of volunteers ready to die for the independence of Quebec. The suicide commandos of the FLQ are aiming principally at the complete destruction, by sabotage, of the colonial institutions, of all means of communication in the colonial language, of the enterprises and commercial firms practising discrimination against the Quebeckers. The FLQ will proceed to eliminate all persons collaborating with the occupant. All the volunteers of the FLQ will carry, during their acts of sabotage, identification papers of the Republic of Quebec. We demand that our wounded and our prisoners be treated according to the statute of political prisoners and according to the Geneva Convention concerning the laws of warfare. The dignity of the people of Quebec requires independence. Students, workers, farmers — form your clandestine groups against Anglo-American colonialism. INDEPENDENCE OR DEATH!

This inflammatory message fell upon deaf ears, for no paper except *Le Devoir* published it, and then only in part. It was circulated clandestinely and printed later in *Les résistants du* FLQ, 1963. We know today that the author of this "Avis à la population" was Georges Schoeters, a Belgian immigrant and former Resistance fighter against the Nazis. This explains the terminology used: "Avis à la population" was the general title of the numerous communications addressed to the population of Belgium by the authorities (and occasionally by the partisans). Expressions such as "occupant," "collaborator," "sabotage," as well as the reference to the Geneva Convention and the laws of warfare clearly point back to the Belgian (and French) Resistance fighters of 1940-1945 who also had — in vain — demanded the protection of the Geneva Convention. The "colonial language" in Belgium had been German; in Quebec it was, of course, English. The cry "Independence or Death" was a copy of Fidel Castro's "Revolución o Muerte." Perhaps because of the lack of publicity for the first pamphlet, two more appeals were launched soon afterwards. They are much too long to be published here, and they do not say anything new, but the last lines of the third pamphlet deserve to be quoted:

QUEBEC PATRIOTS, TO ARMS! THE HOUR OF THE NATIONAL REVOLUTION HAS ARRIVED! INDEPENDENCE OR DEATH!

Again, this "Message to the Nation" was only published in part by the press, but it circulated secretly. Nobody took up arms. On 20 April, 1963, the first FLQ victim died. Several members of the group later explained how the unfortunate accident happened. Gabriel Hudon had made a bomb which was to topple the monument of the Father of the Canadian Confederation, John A. Macdonald, in Dominion Square, Montreal. Jacques Giroux and Yves Labonté wanted to place the bomb near the monument but too many people were around and they decided to go to the Recruiting Centre of the Canadian Army at 772 Sherbrooke Street West. This is quite a busy street, but they found that the lane behind the building was deserted, and placed the time bomb there. It went off around midnight when nobody was supposed to be around, killing the night watchman, Vincent Wilfrid O'Neill, a 65-year-old war veteran who happened to pass through the alley while going to work. One month later, he would have been able to retire on a pension.

The reaction was violent. The three members of the FLQ who had made and placed the bomb were shocked. This, they said, was an unfortunate, unforeseeable accident. According to the great French-Canadian daily *La Presse* it was murder. A number of English-speaking citizens of Quebec seized the Quebec flag and burned it publicly. Mr. Chaput of the Parti républicain expressed the opinion that this was either the work of English *provocateurs* or communists. The English radio station CJMS asked that all separatist parties be outlawed. The death of O'Neill turned public opinion against the FLQ — so much so that some of its members wanted to quit.

André Laurendeau expressed the feelings of the overwhelming majority of French Canadians when he wrote in *Le Devoir,* the day after the death of O'Neill:

> The hidden ones have killed. It had to happen. One does not play with fire unpunished. This time, they've done it. A man has been killed. Whether by error or deliberately, the FLQ have gone the whole way to crime. These are the fireworks of hate.

Laurendeau went on to say that the poor victim did not symbolize anything but a man of the people doing his duty. There was no real courage behind people who set bombs as others sent anonymous letters.

> The hidden ones pretend they are acting in the name of French Canadian nationalism; they do their best to dishonour it. They may be digging the grave of separatism. In front of the murderers and the victim, the French Canadians, whatever their affiliation, are on the side of the victim. . . .
> . . . If I were not convinced that the culprits are sick people, I would be ashamed, for they proclaim they are acting in the name

of us all. In fact, they are alone and they should be made to feel their isolation.

In the meantime, the police of Montreal were inundated with false calls, bomb alarms and irrelevant information concerning the offenders.

Following the death of O'Neill, the FLQ realized that the public was definitely on the side of the victim. After a period of agonizing self-appraisal, they decided to reject the blame for the accident. In doing this, they created a pattern which was to be followed by all the other FLQ groups: never admit a mistake; always put the blame on the "enemy." One of the members wrote a leaflet which was mimeographed, sent to the newspapers and circulated among friends of the organization. It said in part:

> During a nocturnal raid against the recruiting centre of the Canadian Army in Montreal, something unforeseen happened, causing the accidental death of an English-speaking person.* The press of the collaborators immediately spoke of murder and assassination. Unfortunately, no revolution takes place without bloodshed. It would be Utopian to maintain the contrary. While Gandhi was on strike, hundreds of his compatriots were mowed down by British machine-guns. The patriots are not guilty of the death of O'Neill. The guilty ones are all the collaborators, the infamous exploiters who forced the Quebec patriots to take up arms for the liberty of the nation.

In the same pamphlet, the FLQ announced the formation of a "Revolutionary Court of the Quebec Patriots" which would court-martial "the foreign criminals and the Quebeckers betraying their country." If the criminals were found guilty, only one of two sentences could be imposed on them: exile or death.

Finally, still in the same document, the FLQ boasted of having "acquired" the sum of $35,000. They did not say how this money was obtained, but a few days before the National Canadian Bank in Longue Pointe had been held up and robbed of that very amount.

---

* O'Neill had a French-Canadian mother and spoke French besides English.

The next incident was the Solbec Copper Mine affair. The company was undergoing a strike at the time and the FLQ, hoping to regain their lost prestige by proving they were on the side of the workers, decided to scare the big company. On 3 May, 1963, a bomb was placed in the washroom near the Solbec offices. Then an anonymous telephone call was made to the Canadian Press Agency in Montreal urging the evacuation of the premises. This was carried out. The offices were searched but nothing was found and everybody went back to work. In the meanwhile the bomb was ticking away on the floor of the washroom. Fortunately it was discovered in time and was dismantled by Sergeant Plouffe two minutes before it was set to explode.

Again the FLQ sent a communiqué to the press which read:

Friday, a warning was given to Solbec. A bomb was placed near the offices of this company which has become one of the most outstanding examples of the exploitation of the workers by foreign finance. We hope that the warning will have had its effect. Since our patience is not as great as that of the collaborators, we give Solbec one week to settle their differences with the workers to the advantage of the latter. Failing this, we shall be obliged to put the matter into the hands of the Revolutionary Court of the Quebec Patriots.

This ultimatum was published in part in *Le Devoir*. The head of the union concerned, Mr. Emile Boudreau, came out strongly against the interference of the FLQ. In a declaration published in *Le Devoir* of 10 May, he said:

I want to expose the exploitation of our conflict by a small group of irresponsible people who go under the name of FLQ. I would like to think these are mentally ill people and not plain criminals. . . . The FLQ is not informed of the real situation. Solbec does not belong to foreign capital; it is owned by French Canadians.

The authorities began to get concerned. The tourist season was ahead and the bomb scares had to cease. On 8 May, Prime Minister Lesage offered a reward of $10,000 for information leading to the arrest of the terrorists. For their part, the FLQ announced that they received regular subsidies from a professor and had been given $500 by an industrialist. Moreover, a new member had offered a summer camp at St. Faustin, Quebec, as a base.

On 9 May, the Black Watch Armoury at Bleury Street in Montreal was the target of a bomb explosion.

On 17 May, a second person became the innocent victim of an FLQ bomb. The group had decided to "attack" Westmount, symbol of the English establishment, and to place time bombs there in nine different letter boxes. (The boxes, which bear the royal arms with the word "Canada" beneath, were singled out as symbols of foreign occupation.) The bombs were manufactured in a motel in the east end of Montreal, taken to Westmount during the night and placed in the boxes. They were supposed to go off at 3 a.m., but actually only three of them did so; the others either exploded later or were discovered intact at the time of the first clearing. Two were removed by Sergeant Walter Leja, a Polish-born police officer, veteran of the Canadian Army and specialist in bomb disposal. As he was removing his third bomb from one of the boxes there was an explosion which crippled him for life, both mentally and physically.

Again, the FLQ rejected the blame. Moreover, they stated that the "'patriotic" population should not mind, since the victim after all was a representative of the occupying forces.

At about the same time, a group in Quebec City placed eighteen dynamite sticks in letter boxes, to scare the population. These explosives could not go off since they were not provided with a detonator.

The evening before, 16 May, a bomb planted by Jacques Giroux exploded near a big tank of heating oil at the Golden Eagle firm in the east of Montreal. Since the tank was almost empty at the time, the damages were not too great.

The FLQ decided to celebrate Queen Victoria's Birthday, 24 May, with a particularly spectacular coup. Gabriel Hudon fabricated the most powerful bomb to date (75 sticks of dynamite) and with two other members set off for Ottawa with the intention of blowing up the bridge joining the federal capital and Hull, Quebec. Once more, the symbolism of this terrorist plan was evident: destroy all links between Ottawa and Quebec.

When the three approached the bridge they were stopped by two policemen. They had to show their identification papers, after which they were allowed to proceed. Had the policemen been a little more curious they would have examined the package resting on the back seat of the car and discovered a bomb. The three would-be bombers were frightened, however, and returned to Montreal. They were so nervous that they even lost their way. Back in Montreal, they decided to place the bomb near the RCEME building, Grégoire Street, which houses the technical services of the Canadian Army in Montreal. The bomb exploded at 9 a.m. on the Queen's Birthday, with an enormous noise, destroying four cars belonging to French and English citizens living in the vicinity.

The wave of terrorism ended on 1 June. While on the way to place another bomb, three members of the FLQ were arrested by the police. Soon afterwards the bomb-maker was arrested in his home. Several more arrests followed and before the middle of June fifteen people were held pending the first preliminary hearing concerning the death of Wilfrid O'Neill.

Before the last terrorist on the list was arrested he had the time to write one more "Notice to the population of the State of Quebec" and to send it to several newspapers. It was published in facsimile in *Le Devoir* (7 June). The notice was written in the usual inflated language. Here are the main points:

> The suicide commandos of the FLQ just terminated a series of attacks with total success. [Our operations] have shown to the whole world that nothing can stop the march of the Revolution of the Quebec Patriots. The revolution has now become irreversible: nothing can stop it any more. As a matter of fact we have just terminated the complete organization of our structures.
> . . . . .
> The FLQ denounces violently those information media which did

not publish our last manifesto of three pages. This fact once more proves their cowardice before the colonialist exploiter.

. . . . .

INDEPENDENCE OR DEATH

One cannot but be struck by the defiant note of this "manifesto." The author knew that all the others had been arrested and that his turn would come soon. He was indeed arrested on the following day and the "structures" ceased to function.

In order not to warn their accomplices, the first terrorists arrested were kept incommunicado. Even their names were withheld and they were not allowed to see a lawyer at that stage. These tactics were justified by Prime Minister Lesage who pointed out that the prisoners were held at the disposition of the coroner. There was a polemic in *La Presse* as to whether the procedure was legal or not, but the fact is that had the police communicated the names and let them talk to lawyers at the very beginning, the arrest of the other members of the group might have been jeopardized.

Another, perhaps more serious, complaint of several of the prisoners was that they were beaten by the police. The beating up of prisoners who refuse to give pertinent information to the police is unfortunately an old tradition in Quebec. The militants of the first FLQ were not treated worse in this respect than others. Schoeters declared later, "When fourteen years old, I was made a prisoner by the Germans, but they treated me better than the Montreal police." Pierre Schneider was held for days in a cell without a bed, without a chair and without proper light; he could not even wash himself.

It was only after the coroner's inquest was terminated that the prisoners were transferred to better quarters, their names released, and their parents notified.

During the inquest, three men identified themselves as the founders and leaders of the FLQ: Georges Schoeters, a 33-year-old student from Belgium; Raymond Villeneuve, a 22-year-old student; and Gabriel Hudon, a 21-year-old draftsman.

Before the court, some of the defendants displayed great arrogance, refusing to testify at times, demanding to swear on a "revolutionary bible" (such as Fanon's *The Damned of This Earth*), pretending to be before a foreign court having no jurisdiction in Quebec and being judged according to a law they did not recognize. Well aware of the fact that the press of North America was represented in the audience, they used every opportunity to be narcissistic and to disseminate revolutionary propaganda. They even made fun of the coroner; one of the defendants told him on a very hot day, "There is a lot of snow on the other side of the street. Go and refresh yourself there." These antics brought a one-month sentence for contempt of court to several of the defendants. They could not hold up the march of justice, however, and finally all testified to a certain extent and the facts were cleared up. (The bank robbery of $35,000 was attributed to someone else.) *

On 7 October, 1963 Judge Maurice Cousineau pronounced the following sentences**:

Georges Schoeters	12 years	(homicide, O'Neill)
Gabriel Hudon	12 years	(the same)
Raymond Villeneuve	12 years	(the same)
Jacques Giroux	10 years	(the same)
Yves Labonté	6 years	(the same)
Mario Bachand	4 years	(criminal negligence, Leja)
Denis Lamoureux	4 years	(criminal negligence, Leja)
François Gagnon	3 years	(criminal negligence, Leja)
Pierre Schneider	3 years	(criminal negligence)
Jeanne Schoeters	2 years, suspended sentence	
Richard Bizier	6 months	(destruction)
Alain Brouillard	put on probation, promise to guard the peace	
Alain Gabriel	the same	
André Garand	the same	
Gilles Pruneau	jumped bail, was in Algeria	
Eugène Pilote	liberated for lack of proof	

* The behaviour of the main defendants deserves to be noted, because it corresponds to a pattern which became almost general in 1968 after the student riots in the USA, France and Germany, when the defendants did everything they could to make the court look ridiculous.

** On 28 August, 1969, three more partisans of the first FLQ were sentenced. Jean Castonguay, 28; Omer Latour, 28; and Georges Laporte, 30 were sent to prison for four, four, and three years respectively, on charges of possession of dynamite, attempted bank robbery and blowing up a section of a railroad track.

By the end of 1967 even those with the longest sentence had been freed on parole. Mario Bachand subsequently committed another offence: he assaulted some police officers in 1969, after which he sought refuge in Cuba. Georges Schoeters returned to Belgium. Raymond Villeneuve broke the terms of his parole and went to Cuba. Gabriel Hudon remained in Canada. He is married and has two children, but in May 1970 took part in an FLQ hold-up.

Who were these men? What were their alleged and their real motives? What goals did they hope to achieve? What was the outcome? The leaders — Schoeters, Villeneuve and Hudon — we will study in some depth in the following chapter, since by their actions they established certain patterns for their successors to follow. But we can make some observations about the group in general and about some of the individuals in particular.

Of the young men sentenced to prison, two came from broken homes and were not brought up by their parents. A third and a fourth had inadequate, alcoholic fathers. A fifth had lost his mother as a small child and had found it difficult to accept his stepmother. A sixth, the son of a lawyer, grew up in affluence. The other four came from good middle-class families and got along well with their parents.

As far as schooling is concerned, the picture is far from bright. One of the group had hardly any schooling and spoke such bad French that the judge found it hard to understand him. A second had dropped out of school after grade seven. A third had repeated grade ten and then left school. Two were obliged to repeat grade twelve and one, although intelligent, had failed that grade because he rejected the authority of his teachers. Only two had done grade twelve without difficulty.

The intelligence ratings of the group were as follows: below average intelligence 2; average intelligence 2; above average intelligence 6. Of the latter, four were considered to be of superior intelligence, but two of them had had considerable difficulties at school owing to lack of interest, lack of work discipline and too much self-will which made them reject their teachers and the school system. It seems that they rejected school as violently as they later rejected the society in which they had grown up.

Two of the group were married. Both have since been divorced by their wives who kept the children.

Of the group of ten FLQ militants, five were students (four at high school or junior college, one at the university). Four were employed gainfully at the time of their arrest; one was unemployed. Of the four who were working, only one had a stable work record; the others were still trying to find their way.

On the surface the members of the group were not much different from an average sampling of young people in any Canadian metropolis. At least two had grave problems: One had left school too early in order to marry before he was 18, when he already had become a father. (He soon had another child and could not cope with the situation.) The other was handicapped by having left school in grade seven. Several were having difficulties at school and had not yet decided on a profession, but this is an almost normal phenomenon at this age. What seems less normal, of course, is that they had decided to fill the vacuum with a commitment to political violence.

They all had rejected their Roman Catholic faith and in their quest for a new faith had fallen for the kind of political dogmatism which is so well expressed in their tracts. Some of the group were not actually in favour of violence (especially after the first "accident"), but they condoned it.

As for the two who placed the fatal bomb which killed O'Neill (Giroux and Labonté), this is what we know about them: Giroux was 19 years old, the son of a barber-shop owner. He had repeated grade 12 and then taken a private course in photography. He had intended going to Paris in order to study cinematography but had not done so. Though his profession was listed as photographer, he had never worked gainfully at that occupation. (He did, however, carry a camera during the "'raid" on the recruiting centre, posing as a journalist.) Labonté, also 19, had never seen Giroux before they placed the bomb together. He had dropped out of school after grade seven, tried to work as a garage helper, but was found incompetent.

At the time of the O'Neill accident, he was working in a store. He loved adventure and spy stories and was very suggestible. He took part in the FLQ adventure for the "kick" and in order to boost his ego.

A militant of the first FLQ eight years later wrote a character description of the principal members of the group. In this description Schoeters is described as a romantic-mystic who wanted to relive, in the FLQ, his exciting wartime boyhood adventures. (Another friend called him "an exalted person.") Bachand and Schneider are seen as the doctrinaires of the group and as the most fanatic. Villeneuve appears as the man who could not forgive his father for being only a worker.

The first psychiatrist to give his expert opinion on the motives of the young terrorists was André Lussier, a well-known Montreal analyst. His study is all the more remarkable that he wrote it even before the identity of the militants was known. It was published in *Le Devoir* of 5 May, 1963.

Dr. Lussier defined the terrorist as someone who unconsciously apprehends failure as a person. He either cannot or will not play a positive role in society; he is somebody only as far as he is against something. He needs a glamorous revolt and a mystique which allows him to believe that his actions have greatness. The terrorist is a man who cannot wait. He is in a state of mental urgency. Having been unable to resolve his infantile and adolescent conflicts with regard to authority, he needs the illusion of power he gets from attacking the strongest authority, conceived as the strongest enemy. The terror he is able to spread makes him feel he is somebody. Dr. Lussier closed the study with the following statement: "The citizen who, secretly or not, rejoices at the present wave of violence, becomes an accomplice of terrorism."

The Toronto *Globe and Mail,* on 5 June, 1963, published an important editorial pointing out that in Algeria and Ireland similar acts of violence by a comparatively small number of activists had produced a state of chaos because of the passive complicity of numerous groups which, themselves, would never have indulged in violence.

How does one have to interpret the actions of the first FLQ? Which were the real motives? Considering the biographies of the ten terrorists, most of whom had failed in one way or another, the methods of criminality resorted to, and the reactions of the individuals when confronted with their actions, one can say the following:

As a plan to "get rid of the English" the whole enterprise was, as several of the terrorists later admitted, "not very intelligent." It was, in fact, quite puerile. On the other hand, it was also dangerous and harmful to the reputation of the province. The whole conception was a mixture of naïveté and ruthlessness, not to mention criminality. There can be no doubt that these acts of violence appealed to the youthful thirst for adventure, the adolescent need to boost one's ego (*de se valoriser*), the desire to be somebody out of the ordinary and perhaps a hero. Exploding bombs gives, perhaps more than anything else, the feeling of enormous power. To see how the police, the newspapers and the authorities are groping in the dark, searching in the wrong direction and feeling at a loss what to do, gave those terrorists an immense feeling of superiority and satisfaction. Since such feelings were only temporary, the deeds had to be repeated if one wanted to stay in the headlines.

The inflated style of the manifestos, including their presentation (almost a half of the text was in capitals), tells a great deal about the immaturity of the authors. In actual fact those "suicide commandos" were only risking the life of others; the "Court of the Quebec patriots" probably was never in session and certainly never sentenced anyone; those groups of two or three people who, under cover of night, made "an armed attack" were merely quietly placing a time bomb near a building of the "occupying forces." It all seemed a grotesque game of make-believe and sham heroism carried out by young people who "acted like college kids" (as François Gagnon was to say later), allegedly in the name of a great patriotic purpose. There can be no doubt that at least some of the group were convinced that they acted in the interest of the French Canadians, although they used odd means to do so. But none had a real knowledge of the laws governing the political, economic or social life of the people. Their readings were partisan books not conducive to a better understanding of their own motives. Their convictions were not much more than slogans and, quite often, gratuitous assumptions made in the light of their personal experience within the community. Those who had not liked school and rejected the teachers found it easy to reject the authorities and "the system."

After the tragic death of O'Neill, the terrorists were completely isolated. Nobody would have dared to come to their defence at that time. But when Leja became the second victim, the reaction was less violent. After all, he had not died. Yet his fate was as bad as death!

When, at the beginning of June 1963, the terrorists were arrested, a sentimental undercurrent of sympathy and pity began to stir: they were so young, so intelligent, they meant so well — although of course they used the wrong means. Even before they were sentenced two publications were written in their defence: *Les résistants du FLQ* (*The Resisters of the FLQ*) by Bernard Smith, and *La véritable histoire du FLQ* (*The True Story of the FLQ*) by Claude Savoie.

The first book deals extensively with the "resistance" of some of the defendants before the court, *i.e.* with their antics calculated to make the court look ridiculous and to impress the public via the press. The reader was told that these young people "had chosen violence out of love for their country, Quebec," that violence had been used "in the service of a national cause," and that the letters FLQ had become "famous." No use explaining the behaviour of these young people psychologically:

> As usual, the problem is not considered in its real perspective. Wave after wave, one will explain the whole thing by psychological factors: family problems, personality problems, school problems. In short any problem except one: the political problem.

The political problem, Smith explains, is one of stagnation: nothing decisive ever happens to free Quebec of its dependence on the Anglo-Saxons. Thus we have a growing impatience culminating in despair — a despair which will "explode" in the form of bombs and in other acts of violence.

Seen in this perspective, the acts of the first FLQ, which inspired nothing but horror after the death of O'Neill, became patriotic acts of historical significance. We have no longer to do with misguided fanatical nationalists using terrorist methods of intimidation and political blackmail. Those sentenced terrorists had now become patriots, the heralds of a new age, and even the idols of the young generation thirsting for liberty. And the author doubts whether, under the circumstances, their violence could still be called terrorism.

Dr. André Lussier had warned the population that anyone who secretly rejoiced at those acts of violence made himself an accomplice of terrorism. Since the two books cautiously refrained from condemning the violence and tried to explain it in a manner sympathetic to the terrorists, both authors were in a sense "accomplices." Their work bore fruit; the undercurrent of pity and understanding ("He that understands, forgives," says a French proverb) grew visibly. *The True Story of the FLQ* sold over 13,000 copies — a lot for Quebec.

If the problem of the FLQ was not as simple as the authorities saw it, the sympathizers were equally guilty of over-simplifying the issue. The "political question" of Quebec is not how to get rid of the English and Americans, but whether Quebec would be viable as a nation-state.

For centuries, Quebec has rested on two pillars: the French-speaking people who have provided the bulk of labour plus an intellectual élite consisting of professionals, and the English-speaking people who have provided the capital, the business know-how and the work opportunities. In this division of tasks, the English have been privileged. They have had the greater income, the better schools, the better life and this they have justified by the greater role they have played in the economy. Without the English, most people agree, Quebec would have remained industrially dormant, backward like Spain or the south of Italy. To tear the English pillar away by force would be the ruin of Quebec. Yet our terrorists wanted to do just that. And to run headlong out of the American orbit could hardly mean anything else but to run straight into the

Russian zone of influence. We do not even know whether an independent Quebec would be a Western democracy or a "people's democracy," a country ruled dictatorially by a party bureaucracy. The first FLQ certainly had no answer to these basic problems.

Both authors completely overlooked the predominant role, in this outbreak of violence, of the terrorists' thirst for power and prestige and the influence of their romantic ideas of spying and guerrilla warfare. *Certainly, these terrorists wanted independence for Quebec here and now, but only because they wanted freedom from restraints of every kind, be they political, social, or moral.*

The Founders of the FLQ

Georges Schoeters

Because of his age and wartime experience, Georges Schoeters* may be considered the father of FLQ. The "Front de libération québecois" is an imported movement, modelled on the Belgian "résistance" during the second world war, the Algerian National Liberation Front and the Cuban revolution. Schoeters' biography has much to say on that subject.

Georges Schoeters was an illegitimate child who never knew his father. His mother soon became the mistress of a very rich man. She travelled extensively and rarely saw her son. She provided for him financially only. Born on 22 April, 1930 at Antwerp, Georges was raised in an orphanage until Belgium was occupied by the Nazis in 1940. During the occupation he lived with farmers. Twice during the war he was sent to Switzerland for a period of three months, as an asthmatic child.

At the early age of twelve he became acquainted with the partisans who organized the "résistance" in the forests of the Ardennes. Since he was so young and was, moreover, small for his age, Georges made a good messenger and spy; it was unlikely that he would be suspected by the Germans. During the battle of Ardennes in 1944 he fell into the hands of German parachutists but was soon freed by the Americans.

Throughout the whole war, his mother never came to see him. He witnessed sabotage acts — such as the blowing up of a bridge — and heard of all sorts of atrocities. He observed the Belgians defend-

---

* Pronounced *Scooters*.

ing themselves against the Nazis with lies, deceit, fraud, civil disobedience, underground bombs and murder. It is not surprising, therefore, that a young man brought up in these circumstances, who had, moreover, been abandoned by his parents, would have a difficult time after the war in adapting himself to an orderly life in which fraud, sabotage, violence and insurrection were no longer acceptable.

After the war, his mother, attempting to civilize this "savage," boarded him in a classical college. Georges had no trouble with his studies but he did not go further than the fourth grade of the college (ninth grade of schooling). At the age of 17 he declared himself independent and went to Brussels where he worked as office clerk for three years. At that time, he was a member of the Cercle des jeunes travailleurs, a Catholic youth organization. When, at the beginning of 1951, he expressed the wish to emigrate to Canada, one of the leaders of the movement, Abbé Houtard, got in touch with a parish priest in Outremont, Montreal who found a family willing to take him in.

Georges arrived in Canada in September 1951 and immediately became a member of a large French-Canadian family. For the first time in his life (apart from the short periods spent in Switzerland) he had a real family. However, he soon decided that he should learn English and in order to do that left for Vancouver where he worked as a helper in a wayside restaurant. He chose British Columbia because he adored mountains which reminded him of Switzerland, and forests which resembled those of the Ardennes. One year later he returned to Outremont where he had first lived when he came to Canada. He was now fairly fluent in the English language, was 22 years of age and on the lookout for a suitable training or occupation. He was very popular with the children of the family who were all much younger than he, especially when he played ball with them. He thrilled the oldest boy with accounts of his wartime adventures.

For reasons unknown, he had a severe depression toward the end of 1952, and had to be hospitalized. As soon as he got better, he escaped from the institution and came back. He then decided to become an electrician and took his first year course at the trade school. When he had finished this with success, everybody expected him to go in for practical training and finish his apprenticeship with a good firm.

However, Georges decided otherwise. Although he was not especially gifted intellectually, he decided to prepare himself for the university. He was admitted at a classical college and did his pre-university course without too much difficulty. He then left the family and began to study economics and sociology at the University of Montreal. He was helped a great deal by one of his professors and received grants and gifts which allowed him to study. In his free time he worked at the Windsor Station as a helper in the freight department.

When Georges had come to Montreal, he was anything but a revolutionary and still less a nationalist. For him, Quebec was part of Canada and Canada was to be his country. The picture of the Queen hung in his room. He had liked the monarchy in Belgium (which, in a sense, replaced his parents) and he remained a convinced monarchist in Canada for a good ten years.

Even at that time, however, the atmosphere in the Department of Sociology was somewhat nationalistic and it may be that he became influenced by the more militant students there. It seems that he often took part in discussions and that his experience as a freedom fighter gave him a certain prestige. On the other hand, his studies did not advance very rapidly. His academic record shows that it took him six years (till 1959) to get his B.A. in Economics.

On 7 December, 1957, he married a French-Canadian girl from a very good family, an X-ray technician. The marriage took place at the Notre Dame Cathedral in Montreal and was announced on the same day in *La Presse*, together with a picture of the couple. At first, the marriage was quite happy. But soon Georges ruined his chances of a satisfactory home life by running after other interests. He was obviously a restless person, always in search of something new, something better, something different.

Soon after Georges' graduation, Castro, who had just won the revolution in Cuba and who had been markedly slighted by the Washington State Department, came to Montreal. He was received at the Cercle social of the University of Montreal and Schoeters was among those who greeted him. Castro invited the students to come to Cuba and help with agrarian reform. Georges put aside his studies and, together with his wife, went to Cuba. He was motivated to go by idealism and by a sincere desire to help the people. He was very impressed by the stark misery of the peasants.

Since his wife was pregnant, Georges soon sent her back to Montreal. And after serving about a year in Cuba, he also returned. I have heard from several of his friends that he came back somewhat disappointed. Castro had not looked so glamorous on closer inspection. His aides were already strongly under Russian influence (except Ché Guevara) and did not have the lofty ideals Georges had taken for granted. He found that progress was painfully slow and that the reality was not up to the slogans which covered the walls.

Georges did not remain long with his family. In 1961 he visited Rome, Tunisia, Turkey, Algeria and Switzerland. In Algeria he was in touch with the National Liberation Front.

After these two formative years, he was well equipped to import the revolution to Quebec. He became a member of the Rassemblement pour l'indépendance nationale (the RIN which dissolved in 1968), which he did not find radical enough. He then formed the Réseau de résistance (RR) which was inspired by the Belgian Resistance but which was content for the moment to paint slogans on walls. Finally, part of the RR split away and called itself "Front de libération québecois," commonly called FLQ. Like its Belgian, Algerian and Cuban models, this was to be an underground movement devoted to defeating the English "occupant" by violence. The enemy was the monarchy and the confederation, which they attacked by damaging government buildings and military establishments, and by trying to derail the Prime Minister's election-campaign train.

The group was composed of about fifteen members. They met in Schoeters' apartment on Côte des Neiges (His wife fully approved of the FLQ scheme), or in a restaurant, or at Lamoureux's place. Schoeters had brought instructions from Algeria for the making of Molotov cocktails and time bombs. Gabriel Hudon made first cocktails and then bombs. Villeneuve wrote and canvassed new members. The others had secondary functions: spying out the locations, standing on guard while a project was being carried out, etc. Mrs. Schoeters was particularly useful in keeping watch at the location of a bomb attempt, as nobody suspected a woman of terrorist activity at that time.

Schoeters did not participate personally in the dynamite thefts, nor in the fabrication of bombs. His role was more in the nature of co-ordinator. The dynamite was apparently stolen by Raymond Villeneuve, Gabriel Hudon, Roger Tétreault and Richard Bizier, and transported by taxi to Schoeters' apartment. However, because of Mrs. Schoeters' objections, the explosives were soon taken to a forest near St. Faustin. It seems that only Villeneuve knew the exact three hiding places.

It is surprising that young people of 20 years of age who had never been employed in construction, were able to get hold of 382 sticks of dynamite plus the necessary detonators almost as easily as if they had been buying so many cigarettes. At that time, the Métro* was being built and the dynamite was stored on the construction site, badly guarded (Who thought of stealing dynamite then?), and in such a large quantity that a theft was not immediately noticeable. It seems that a small boy of ten was sometimes used to steal the dynamite sticks; he could easily clamber in and out through the air vents. The bombs used by Schoeters and his companions were made of from two to ten sticks each; their cache of dynamite thus sufficed for at least forty bombs.

The first FLQ team not only planted bombs, they held discussions. Schoeters gave glowing accounts of the Cuban and Algerian revolutions. Many of the members of the group read a great deal and it is not without interest to notice that their reading material was not confined to detective stories or terrorist pamphlets. Here is an incomplete list of books which circulated in the group: Fanon's *The Damned of This Earth* (called the bible of the Algerian National Liberation Front), Marcuse's *Soviet Marxism*, Kafka's *The Castle*, Camus' *The Rebel*, various writings by Bertrand Russell and Toyn-

* Montreal subway.

bee, and the biographies of Lenin, Trotsky, Hitler, Goering and other revolutionaries.

In the penitentiary, Schoeters at one time staged a hunger strike. Then he became a model prisoner who studied a lot. He suffered enormously from being separated from his family. The FLQ adventure had left a deep mark on him; it was the greatest disappointment in his life. Quebec had obviously not been ready for liberation. They had failed to rally the people to their cause. The friends who had paid for his trip to Algeria avoided him. His wife soon stopped visiting. He was not subject to deportation, since he already had become a Canadian citizen, but he could only get parole on condition that he sign a promise to leave the country. Apparently Belgium was ready to take him back and he agreed to go. Two weeks before his departure his wife obtained an annulment of her ten-year-old marriage. He could not say good-bye to her nor to his children. It was a very lonely man who took the plane to Brussels on Christmas Eve, 1967.

Thanks to the help of his (non-revolutionary) friends, Georges had been able to write his M.A. thesis in the penitentiary. Its title is *Les effets des accords internationaux sur les produits de base, 1950-1960 (The Effects of International Agreements on the Basic Products, 1950-1960)*. It is a work of 300 pages, extremely objective, free of anti-capitalist overtones. It is true that the author points out different attempts of certain monopolistic enterprises to create artificial shortages in order to raise prices, but he also shows that these efforts met with no success. The problem of overproduction was much more serious and had to be dealt with by international agreements.

The thesis, dated August 1966, was accepted and Georges Schoeters was handed his diploma when leaving the penitentiary, in December 1967. It had taken him eight years from the B.A. to the M.A.

It is not quite clear what happened to Schoeters in the years that followed. The information I have obtained from different sources is conflicting. One thing is certain: The carefully thought-out plan which provided that he was to study economics and sociology at the

(Flemish) University of Louvain under the supervision of Abbé Houtard did not work. Apparently Schoeters could not get permission to stay in Louvain, quite apart from the fact that the university refused him entry on the grounds that the courses had begun some time before. At that time the university was the centre of violent clashes between Flemish and French-speaking Belgians and it seems that the authorities did not want a man with a terrorist past to stay in Louvain at all. For some time after that, Schoeters lived clandestinely in Brussels. Later he was in Prague, where the authorities again considered him an undesirable. He turned up in Paris before the student revolt in the spring of 1968, but did not want to be cast in the role of an experienced revolutionary by a bunch of Quebec students there. A Parisian lawyer advised him to go to Switzerland and apply for political asylum.

Schoeters had friends in Switzerland. He contacted Mr. Neukomm, a factory owner, and his wife who agreed to offer their hospitality to this man who was practically a fugitive. Schoeters also made his request for political asylum. It was an unfortunate move. Had he simply applied for a labour permit he might have been allowed to stay without much difficulty, for Switzerland badly needed foreign labour. As it was, Schoeter's request went to Berne and the wheels of the federal bureaucracy began to turn. After a few months, his life story was known to the *police des étrangers* and in 1969 the Swiss government decided to withdraw his permit to stay in Switzerland. Schoeters appealed the decision with the help of a lawyer from Geneva, but was turned down on 20 August, 1969. He may not enter Switzerland, where he has his best friends, for ten years.

It is not known for certain where Schoeters went from there. It is probable, however, that he returned to Brussels where he has a few friends. In the summer of 1970 he turned up in Stockholm. He is working there as a helper in a pharmacy. He has declared several times that he has had enough of revolution to last him for the rest of his life.

If Georges Schoeters returns to Canada (the only country which must accept him), he would have to finish eight years of penitentiary, since one of the conditions for parole was that he stay in

Belgium. Schoeters declared in Switzerland that Canada was the last country he would go to. Yet this may be the only possibility left. He is still being punished for his romantic revolutionary illusions which he lost long ago. For nineteen of his twenty adult years he has been living at the expense of someone else.

Schoeters' fate was to be rejected again and again: by his father and mother, by his wife, by his native country and by all those countries in which he tried to settle. In contrast to his young friends who loved adventure and were staging a kind of exciting revolutionary romance, Georges Schoeters had — and still has — very profound reasons for hating society and feeling alienated from it. In 1963, he sincerely believed in the necessity and in the future of an independent Quebec. He had lacked maternal affection as a child, had been handicapped by the absence of a valid father figure and had been acquainted as a young boy with the tyranny and cruelty of a foreign occupying power which could only be fought by violence. He was really a cosmopolitan, but his love of adventure and his need to play a role made him opt for the romantic sham heroism of the FLQ. His wife described him as a man with a dream and an eternal student.

Raymond Villeneuve

Together with Georges Schoeters, Raymond Villeneuve is to be considered as one of the principal leaders of the 1963 terrorism in Quebec. He is a young man with an athletic build and above-average intelligence. He is an activist in the true sense of the word, since he immediately transforms ideas into action. Extremely impatient, he cannot wait for anything. He is characterized by an extremely tenacious will. He knows what he wants and cannot bear a single objection or failure or frustration.

In 1963, he was 19 years old but he looked older and more mature. When he was in grade twelve, he had already begun to grow impatient. Studying was not taking action. To reflect was not to be accomplishing anything. He showed considerable promise as a student and one of his teachers at St. Stanislas High School in Outremont wrote: "Raymond Villeneuve goes to our school. I commend him for his good behaviour, his seriousness and his general attitude. Raymond is also president of the Ralliement des jeunes Canadiens français, a group consisting of young people interested in our social problems."*

Feeling that his mother was not allowing him enough freedom and translating his personal thirst for independence into desire for the independence of Quebec, he became at first a member of the RIN, then of the RR, writing slogans on walls. More than Schoeters, he was exasperated by the lack of immediate success in both of these movements. He was eager to pass on to a more direct and spectacular kind of action. In RIN and RR, he met Schoeters and Gabriel Hudon. It was Villeneuve who, having heard the Belgian's vivid stories about the Belgian Resistance, the Algerian Liberation Front and the Cuban revolution, proposed the name of "Front de libération québecois" for the terrorist group. He even designed a flag, following the example of the Viet Cong. The flag was in the French colours: one vertical half blue, one white, with a red star in the white portion.

The targets of the group were the armed forces of Canada, the monarchy, government buildings and "establishments which exploit the people of Quebec." Raymond's job was to look after the organization and the recruitment of new members. From the very beginning this was to be a secret society, without a list of members and divided into cells of three people. The members of one cell knew each other but they often were only known to members of other cells by first-name pseudonyms such as "Jean," André," etc. In this way, if the members of one cell were arrested, it would be impossible to get a single name from them which might lead the police to another cell. This procedure was copied from that of the wartime Resistance fighters.

Nothing in Raymond's family history influenced him to become a revolutionary. He was born on 11 September, 1943, the oldest son of a French-Canadian pastry maker, foreman in a factory. He had two brothers and two sisters. He is the only extremist in this peaceful, hardworking and very respected middle-class family. Raymond

* Quoted from Smith, *Les Résistants du FLQ*, p. 15.

finished St. Stanislas High School. In grade twelve he had an average grade of 69% but failed in chemistry, a failure which unfortunately prevented his admission to university. He worked from time to time in the same firm as his father, but soon devoted himself full-time to political action. It was he, who, with others, stole the dynamite from the Métro construction site. He also admitted later that he had thrown the Molotov cocktails into military establishments. Arrested at the beginning of June 1963, he was found guilty of manslaughter by a jury presided over by Judge Cousineau, and was sentenced to twelve years' imprisonment.

In court, Raymond displayed a superb revolutionary arrogance. Like Schoeters, Hudon and Giroux, he often refused to testify. In prison, he adapted himself quite well and studied a great deal. In August 1967 he was able to pass the entrance exams at the Ecole des hautes études commerciales of the University of Montreal. On 14 September of that year, the Parole Board in Ottawa freed him so that he would be able to attend the courses which were to begin on 18 September. The society which he had wanted to destroy thus gave him another chance. In return, he declared that he did not want to have anything more to do with violence and that the FLQ had gone much too far.

Unfortunately, Raymond was not suited for commercial studies. He failed in an examination. Soon he began taking courses in sociology — the field of studies which attracts so many malcontents, contesters and rebels, and which can supply all the sociological theories and value systems desired. Exposed to this atmosphere, it seems that Raymond became more extreme. On top of that, he also had an unhappy love affair. Betraying the trust of the authorities and under the influence of another ex-terrorist and extremist, he left for Mexico at the beginning of 1968 and from there went to Cuba.

In Cuba, Raymond is anything but a free man. He has to cut sugar whenever requested (extremely arduous physical labour performed under a pitiless sun), he has to live in quarters allotted to him, his letters are censored (as in jail), his food is severely rationed (as is everybody's), he gets meat only twice a week, he has very little choice in his studies, and he cannot leave the country without

Castro's permission. He speaks Spanish fluently and soon will have learned everything there is to be learned under the circumstances. If Canada imposed such restrictions on her citizens, they would be considered intolerable. (It seems that he left Cuba in the summer of 1970.)

I think that Villeneuve might have broken his parole conditions because he could not stand the idea that he should ask for permission if he wanted merely to spend a holiday in the United States; he would have been too proud to do that. Moreover, the conditions of parole came from Ottawa and he does not recognize the jurisdiction of any federal agency. It is possible also that he originally intended only to go to the USA and then realized that if he returned he might have to go back to jail. (These explanations were suggested to me by some of his friends.)

Indeed, if Raymond does return to Canada, he must serve the rest of his sentence — eight years. Therefore, he will return only if Quebec becomes independent. This seems to be one of those special cases where an amnesty might be in order.

Here we have another young man who, of his own wish, has alienated himself from his family, his country, and the society in which he grew up and to which he owes his education. Revolution is not liberation; it is tyranny. The example of Georges Schoeters and Raymond Villeneuve, the founders of the FLQ, seems to prove that a man, once he enters the orbit of revolutionary obsession, no longer remains the master of his actions and still less of his destiny.

Gabriel Hudon

Gabriel Hudon, born on 1 March, 1942, in Montreal, was the third member in importance of the FLQ team of 1963. He has four brothers and a sister. One of his brothers was a prison guard; his brother-in-law is a merchant. His father, a stevedore, died in 1967. The boy was traumatized by the fact that his father was an alcoholic and indifferent to the fate of his children.

Gabriel, though intelligent, quit school at the end of grade eleven because he wanted to work and become independent. While working all day as delivery boy or cashier at a grocery store, he took a night course in mechanical drawing and soon found a good job as drafts-man. At the time of his arrest, he had kept this job for two years.

In 1963, Hudon was very active in the FLQ, where he went by the name of "Roger Dupuis." He participated in the dynamite thefts and was involved in most of the violent activities. He was charged on ten separate counts. Like Villeneuve, who was a year younger than he, Gabriel showed much contempt for the court and the authorities. On 7 October, he was sentenced to twelve years of imprisonment for the manslaughter of O'Neill. He also was sentenced to five years for each count (nine in all) for damages to various buildings. The ten terms were to be served concurrently.

In prison, he read a lot, especially economics, sociology and politics. He was freed on parole three months after Villeneuve, on 11 December, 1967. In contrast to the latter, he kept the conditions of his parole for a long time. He married and had two children. Unfortunately, he lost his job and in May 1970 took part in a hold-up.

Most of the fifteen partisans of the first FLQ came from a rather modest background, but few had experienced real hardships. One of the members, François Gagnon, was the son of a lawyer. (His brother Jean was later involved in FLQ activities.)

After the arrests, Isocrate, in an article in *Le Devoir*, 6 July, 1963, warned the public that this would not be the end. "Beside those FLQ members who were before the court, there are other victims, to various degrees, of patriotic illuminism, who are already engaged — and who are making military preparations — to stage the Battle of the Plains of Abraham again with the opposite results. . . . In their revolutionary mysticism, they know that there will be victims. They expect this. Not to combat by force an army of three united police forces, but to 'stimulate' the separatist chiefs, to 'strain' the situation, to intimidate responsible politicians and manipulate public opinion. There will be other explosions, other attacks, other threats: at least to accelerate the march to independence."

In other words, the partisans of the FLQ, like the leaders of the anarchist wave which hit England and Russia in the 1880's, believed in "propaganda by deed." As Hitler pointed out in *Mein Kampf*, a revolutionary movement, in order to get off the ground, very much needs the free publicity it gets in the press thanks to its illegal acts.

It is interesting to note how events looked to the first members of the FLQ in retrospect. Pierre Schneider, out on parole, and Raymond Villeneuve, who was still in prison, were interviewed on the French radio station CJMS (November 1967). Schneider was presented as a journalist, while Villeneuve's name was not mentioned. Villeneuve explained that the political parties did not seem able to establish independence, that the RIN was the most serious of separatist parties and that it should channel the energies of the young in order to prevent them from rushing into actions which would not produce anything.

Asked what might have stopped him in 1963 from becoming a terrorist, Villeneuve answered candidly: "A little more experience." Then the interviewer asked him about the role of parents. Villeneuve deplored the lack of dialogue between parents and children. Parents, he said, often lacked any political affiliation and held ideas which created a gap between them and their children.

Then Villeneuve made the following statement concerning the young eager for political action: "They should think it over before going in for actions which end in deadlock." Obviously speaking of himself, he said that young people expected "all sorts of things" from a terrorist movement. He also said he would not begin again; the secrecy and incarceration had been very hard to bear and too high a price to pay.

The interview with Villeneuve was followed by an interview with Dr. Karl Stern, psychiatrist and analyst of social problems. He said that the terrorists often acted from unconscious motives, that the roots of their present behaviour might lie in early childhood (generally due to some kind of rejection). He said also that the young were fascinated by danger and violence and were not aware that it was personal problems which prompted them to act as they did. Dr. Stern did not believe that violence could bring any solution for Quebec's problems. On the other hand, he thought that the most violent of the young terrorists were perhaps those who were the most amenable to treatment and cure. He called them adolescents and explained that adolescence was a chaotic phase.

Then the interviewer said that the station had conducted a survey with 2,000 young French Canadians. Of these, only 10% approved of violence as a political weapon. The great majority (89%) were absolutely against the use of violence to solve political problems. Eighteen per cent had never heard of the FLQ. But one young man had said, "For me, these people are heroes. Yet I conceive independence together *with* the English, the Americans and the Jews, contrary to the FLQ."

Pierre Schneider, too, was very "reasonable" on his radio interview. Yet only six months before, he had written in a letter, presumably smuggled out of prison, "For a real revolutionary, anything is moral which accelerates the emancipation of the colonized masses."

The End of the First FLQ

At one time, twenty-five persons were arrested in connection with the FLQ bombings. Of these, only fifteen were actually connected with the Schoeters group.

According to Smith: *Les Résistants du FLQ*, the first FLQ had justified the use of violence for political ends as follows:

1. The revolutionary movement is the consequence of colonialism. The passive and subtle violence to which the people are subjected produces sooner or later a violence of the people against its exploiters.

2. The enemy is too powerful.

3. Our politicians look after their own interests.

4. We do not use violence in the name of some ideology, but in order to open the way for the development of man and the emancipation of the working class.

5. Violence is the only possible way of overthrowing colonialism.

The aim of violence is "the liberation of man"; violence is therefore a form of "love for man." (I have been told this was written by 18-year-old Pierre Schneider. It bears, at any rate, that stamp of absolutism which is characteristic of an older adolescent.)

As we have seen, the first wave of FLQ terrorism was based on an ultra-nationalist and Marxist ideology. The province of Quebec was cast in the role of an occupied country comparable to Nazi-occupied

France or Belgium, or put on the same level as the French or British colonies which, one after the other, had become free. The Quebec workers were seen as exploited colonized masses who were not even aware of their predicament. As Villeneuve said in his radio interview of November 1967, the workers "enjoy a relative prosperity" which gives them the "illusion of not being exploited."

By throwing Molotov cocktails and by placing bombs, the first FLQ expected to awake the workers and to create a pre-revolutionary situation — a climate of unrest, insecurity and fear in which the authorities would gradually lose control. As we shall see, the other waves had much the same aim.

The exalted (not to say hysterical) language used in the first "proclamations" was, of course, inspired by wartime experiences, then by the experiences and writings of professional revolutionaries, and finally by the different "liberation fronts" in Algeria, Guatemala, Cuba, etc. Since the situation of Quebec could not possibly be compared to that of Nazi-occupied France or to Algeria, it had to be dramatized out of all proportion. Things had to look so absolutely intolerable that a violent change was in order.

There is one classical example for this procedure: Germany after the first world war. Hitler could not accept German defeat and still less its outcome, the Treaty of Versailles. It took him ten long years to convince the German people that this treaty *was* intolerable, that Germany *was* in chains, that the Versailles Treaty and the Jews *were* responsible for all the ills. ("The Jews are sucking German blood.") In actual fact, the Treaty of Versailles was quite humane and, moreover, subject to amendments. After the second world war, East Germany alone, with a population of 13 million, paid, without complaints, far greater sums to Soviet Russia than the Treaty of Versailles had ever imposed on the whole of Germany which had a population of 60 million people.

What helped Hitler in the end was the great depression of the thirties. During that time, Germany could not meet her payments. The misery among the unemployed masses was great and Hitler exploited it to the full, explaining that it was the infamous, unjust Treaty and the exploitation by the Jews which produced the unemployment. Hitler's contestation of the "regime" was successful and we all know about the new world that followed. One wonders what would have happened to Quebec if the Quebec workers had not enjoyed relative prosperity and if the FLQ contestation had been successful. The FLQ could not succeed because its basis was much too small and because conditions were not so intolerable as they painted them.

As we shall see, the subsequent waves of terrorism were based on very much the same ideology of a colonized country to be liberated. The revolutionaries drew their inspiration from Marxist sources (They think very much in terms of class war which, here, also becomes a war between French and Anglo-Saxons), from Camus' book *The Rebel* (*L'homme révolté*, 1962) which is a philosophical justification of revolt and violence, from Fanon's *The Damned of This Earth* and later from Marcuse and from Pierre Vallières' *White Negroes of America*. The general wave of confrontation and student revolt sweeping the world. From 1963 to 1968 also could only serve to reinforce the revolutionary fervour of the later FLQ partisans.

The Second Wave

September 1963-April 1964

From 2 June to 26 September, 1963, there were no more acts of terrorism. Then, just before the day of sentencing the partisans of the first FLQ, other terrorists entered the ranks. The second wave lasted from 26 September, 1963 to 9 April, 1964. Like the first wave, it ended abruptly with the arrest of the partisans who "worked" for a liberating army of Quebec, "L'Armée de libération du Québec" (ALQ). This time, there were no bombs, but considerable thefts of arms, ammunition, military equipment and, above all, bank hold-ups. The following is a chronicle of these events:

On 26 September, 1963 there was an armed hold-up at the Royal Bank at 5301 Sherbrooke West, Montreal, during which $6,929 was stolen. (It was learned later that the members of the gang used this money to motorize in great style.)

On 26 November, 1963 a burglary took place at the CHEF radio station in Granby. A radio transmitter and other radio equipment to a total value of $4,000 was taken. (It has never been established that this was the work of the ALQ.)

On 16 January, 1964 there was a hold-up in a Montreal military establishment during which $1,640 was pilfered.

On 30 January, 1964 there was a hold-up at the Fusiliers of Mount Royal Armoury in Montreal. Military equipment (arms, ammunition, telescopes, etc.) to the value of $20,000 was stolen.

On 20 February, 1964 guns and ammunition to the value of $21,000 was stolen from the armoury of the 62nd Regiment of the Royal Canadian Artillery at Shawinigan.

On 27 February, 1964 a hold-up involving the theft of $9,000 took place at the Caisse Populaire at l'Assomption near Shawinigan.

On 23 March, 1964 there was a hold-up at the Caisse Populaire Hochelaga in Montreal that yielded $17,475.

On 26 March, 1964 in a hold-up at the Provincial Bank at Rosemere $23,000 was taken.

On 9 April, 1964 there was a hold-up at the Canadian National Bank at Mont Rolland during which $5,000 was stolen. On the same day, the group was arrested.

The outcome of these events was dramatic: the leader of the group was none other than the younger brother of terrorist Gabriel Hudon, who had been imprisoned since 17 October, 1963. Robert Hudon was a 19-year-old apprentice electrician. His accomplices were: Jean Gagnon, 22 (elder brother of François Gagnon of the first FLQ); Jean Lasalle, 21; Pierre Nadon, 18; Claude Perron, 19; and André Wattier, 23. Within six months this group had stolen $40,000 in cash, plus military and electronic equipment to the value of $55,000. The equipment was found intact but most of the money had been spent, for the gang lived in high style. Robert Hudon alone owned two trucks and one car; and the Bureau of Motor Vehicles had never posed the question as to how a 19-year-old apprentice electrician could pay for such luxury!

Imitating the example of his older brother, Robert Hudon was also very arrogant in front of the judge. He seemed to take it as a personal affront to be treated like a common thief. Yet he and his companions had lived, and lived well, on the proceeds of their robberies. He explained that the military and electronic equipment was stolen to get the ALQ off the ground. But, this "army" had not a single soldier, no headquarters, no strategy, no uniforms. The six conspirators had lived a real life of adventure, reminiscent of that of the high sea pirates of the sixteenth and the seventeenth centuries as described in boys' books. It seems that the liberation of Quebec had only been a pretext to give free rein to those romantic criminal tendencies which may lurk in many people, and to satisfy their thirst for adventure and personal independence. The clandestine journal of the FLQ, *La Cognée*, later made heroes of "Robert Hudon and his soldiers," but today there are not many ex-terrorists who would think that way.

Robert Hudon was sentenced by Judge Sylvestre to eight years' imprisonment for two (!) armed robberies. He was freed on parole in December 1967, about the same time as his brother Gabriel. For a number of years he has been drinking and his friends were reluctant to talk about him. He was to be in the limelight again in 1970.

His accomplices got the following sentences from the same judge:

Jean Gagnon, 22	8 years
Jean Lasalle, 21	8 years
Claude Perron, 20	2 years
André Wattier, 23	8 years
Pierre Nadon, 19	2 years

Robert Hudon was the youngest of his family. Like his brother Gabriel, he felt rejected by his father.

The ALQ group was not very homogeneous. One member was the son of a lawyer, another the son of a medical doctor. None of the six had really been underprivileged. Most of them had very good manners. There were no hirsute or hippy types among them. During the robberies in the armouries, they were courteous to the guards they had tied to chairs, offering them cigarettes and exchanging jokes. The students among them had interrupted their studies to stage a revolution.

One thing was proven, though: how vulnerable those military establishments were. It is surprising that Quebec has no less than sixty-seven such armouries, each of them crammed full with expensive military equipment. This decentralization of valuable but actually unused material is, of course, a heritage of the time when transportation was by horse and cart and when armies marched on foot from one place to another. From the point of view of safety as well as for financial reasons, it would seem that this way of storing military equipment is outmoded.

The Third Wave

The Schirm hold-up, August 1964

After Robert Hudon and his accomplices were arrested, and the considerable amount of military equipment which they had stolen and stored was confiscated, the Armée de libération du Québec ceased to exist before it had been able to train a soldier. But, there were other young men who felt called upon to follow suit.

One of these was François Schirm, an immigrant of Hungarian origin and a former sergeant in the French Foreign Legion, who was converted to the cause of the FLQ. The extraordinary background of this man will be told later. For the moment we shall sketch the violent episode which characterized this third wave of violence. The activity of Schirm's group centered around an embryonic Armée révolutionnaire du Québec, a formation formally approved by the regional chief of the FLQ. This "army" established a training camp near St. Boniface, Quebec, consisting of a few camping tents and a hunting cabin near a lake. In August 1964, a dozen recruits were being drilled there. One part of the training was to drill men for political demonstrations in Montreal, but some were also told they might have to fight the provincial police with arms. The recruits were informed that similar camps were to be set up all over the province. One of the recruits was Jean-Guy Lefebvre, who was 25 years old and who was to appear on the scene again in November 1965 when he was the leader of a gang of seven who "kidnapped" two policemen near La Tuque. Moreover, on 24 June, 1969, he was one of the demonstrators who, like Herodias, "beheaded" the statue of St. John, patron saint of Quebec, at the end of the St. John the Baptist parade in Montreal.

The St. Boniface training camp was lacking in everything — food, guns, ammunition, money. FLQ members had promised to supply all this, but nothing arrived. Because of this situation, François Schirm decided to take things into his own hands. With the approval of the FLQ regional group, he organized an armed robbery to take place at the International Firearms gunshop, at 1011 Bleury Street in Montreal. The plan was carried out on Saturday, 29 August, 1964, at 4:50 p.m. The result: there were two deaths; Schirm and his accomplices were put behind bars; and the St. Boniface camp was invaded by the police. This marked the end of the third wave.

The facts behind the hold-up, which are known in detail, are not without interest. Those involved were called together the day before. Schirm explained the general plan to them and distributed the roles. None of the participants had ever been involved in armed or unarmed robbery before, but they knew about hold-up techniques from FLQ instructors. Only one of them had taken part in illegal FLQ activities before. Everyone seemed to be excited by the prospect of taking part in an act of patriotism at the expense of a store which, they noticed, did not even bother to have a French name. No one seemed to understand how serious the affair was; only Gilles objected to the use of weapons.

On Saturday afternoon, the conspirators once again met at 2565 Davidson Street, Apartment 2. Cyr wanted to participate only on condition that he would just be the chauffeur and would not have to enter the store. This was accepted. Gilles, seeing how things were going, wanted to back out, but apparently Schirm threatened him with reprisals if he did so. With a heavy heart, Gilles went to play the part which was assigned to him. Meanwhile, a thief was hired to steal a car; he soon arrived with a brand-new Pontiac. It was to be used to transport the loot to a predetermined spot where the arms would be transferred to another vehicle which would bring them to St. Boniface. The stolen Pontiac would be abandoned. These details are interesting: they show that the procedure followed was that of professional hold-up men.

At 4 o'clock they got into the Pontiac. Edmond Guénette, 20 years old and a full-time activist of the FLQ for three months, was armed with a loaded rifle containing fifteen cartridges. The others were unarmed. The five of them arrived at the corner of Craig and Bleury Streets. Since it was too early for the hold-up, which was scheduled for 4:50, they went to a tavern where a few beers each helped to make them more enterprising and more carefree. With military precision, the hold-up men arrived in front of the gunshop ten minutes before closing time. Schirm gave Gilles a revolver and ordered him to go to the office upstairs and to make the secretary come down so that she would not be able to use the telephone. Gilles told him that he had never had a revolver in his hand and did not know how to use it. Schirm is said to have replied, "Do what you're told. The revolver is not loaded, so you won't be able to shoot us in the back."

The manager of the store and Vice-President of the company had the very British name of Leslie MacWilliams. It was he who died, at the age of 56, at the hands of a 20-year-old fanatic who was burning with justice for Quebec. The tragedy of such a situation is that it does not seem to be possible to establish justice without inflicting the greatest injustice on those who do not share your views.

The Pontiac, still with its Quebec licence number (488-348), was parked in the lot reserved for customers. As agreed, Cyr stayed at the wheel. François went into the store and asked to see a 30 MI rifle. Before the sales clerk was able to realize what was happening, Schirm exchanged the empty magazine of the rifle for a full one which he took out of his pocket. Now armed with a loaded rifle, he ordered the employee to keep still. Gilles came in and went up to the second floor where he got the secretary to come down after taking her glasses off. Halfway down, he heard a shot and saw a man lying on the ground, groaning. What had happened? While Schirm was "covering" the sales clerk, Edmond had come in with his loaded gun. At the same time, the Vice-President of the company had arrived on the scene to see what was happening. Edmond pointed his gun at him. Thinking this was a bad joke on the part of a juvenile (Edmond is very small and looked younger than his age), MacWilliams asked him to please lower his gun. He had hardly finished the sentence when a shot put an end to his life. He was shot through the abdomen and died of internal hemorrhage. There was no more resistance. The three accomplices gathered up weapons and boxes of ammunition and took them to the car, while François and Edmond kept watch on the employees.

By a curious coincidence, a false alarm had brought the police to a nearby store. The policemen, finding nothing wrong, left and passed by International Firearms on their way back. Precisely at that moment, one of Mr. MacWilliams' employees, who had managed to leave the store, signalled to the patrol. Marcel had just time to alert Schirm that the police had arrived. Schirm fired a few shots in the air to keep them at a distance. They fired back. Alfred Pinisch, a 37-year-old German immigrant and father of two children, emerged from the workshop with a gun in his hand. He was mistaken for a thief and shot by a policeman. Pinisch, a gunsmith and rifle-shooting champion of Quebec, had heard what was going on. He could have stayed in the workshop at the back of the store, but had wanted to defend his employer's property.

François and Edmond fled through the front door. Not much later, Schirm was found and arrested in a shed where he was hiding. He was wounded and taken to hospital under heavy guard. Edmond took a taxi. Threatening the taxi driver with his gun, he had himself driven to Rosemount free of charge. A few days later, the police arrested him at the training camp of the Armée révolutionnaire du Québec. The police also arrested Marc-André Parisé, 20, leader and cook of the camp; Jean-Guy Lefebvre, 25 (of whom we have heard before); Yves Husserault, 18; Claude Nadeau, 21; Louis-Philippe Aubert, 20; and Bernard Mataigne, 20. They were freed on 12 November of a charge of conspiring to stage an armed robbery.

On 10 December, however, Bernard Mataigne pleaded guilty to a charge of possession of explosives and was given a suspended sentence. He later worked for the Company of Young Canadians in Montreal, then for a movement called "Libération populaire," together with Stanley Gray.

After they were arrested, two of the accomplices, who were particularly shocked by the tragic turn of events and wanted to make a clean breast of it, confessed what they had done. Cyr seems to have been the most uncooperative; his attitude in front of the court was such that he received two extra years for refusing to testify in the case of Schirm and Guénette. It is hard to see what his obstinate silence was to attain, as the facts of the case were already sufficiently known. He would explain later that he was afraid of retaliation.

During the preliminary inquiry, as well as during the trial, the partisans of the group maintained that they had had absolutely no intention of killing anyone. Their whole goal had been to get the arms, ammunition and money needed to train the Quebec guerillas. All of them had been more or less convinced that only an armed struggle could liberate Quebec.

The members of Schirm's group received extremely severe sentences. On 21 May, 1965, François Schirm and Edmond Guénette were sentenced to death for the capital murder of Leslie MacWilliams. The date of execution was set for 22 October, 1965. The case was appealed. This happened at a time when, after Jacques Hébert's book on the Coffin case, Canadian public opinion no longer approved of the death penalty. Guénette had sworn that the mortal bullet had been fired from his gun but that it had been an accident. Delisle, Brunet and Tardif got a life sentence.

It should be remembered that the perpetrators of the first wave of terrorism (which claimed one dead and one invalid) had got away with eight to twelve years of imprisonment.

During the second trial, which ended on 10 October, 1967, Schirm and Guénette were sentenced to life imprisonment for noncapital murder.

After the sentence was pronounced, the prisoners were on their own. The movement for which they had worked could not support them in any way. Cyr, Marcel and Gilles said they preferred to be in a different institution than Schirm.

The members of Schirm's group were young people of rather modest background. There was no intellectual among them. Four of the five had had experiences in which the Anglophones had treated French Canadians as naturally inferior.

The biography of the leader, François Schirm, is extremely instructive. It resembles in some points that of Schoeters, with the exception that Schirm has absolutely no cause for blaming his parents. The collaboration of both Schirm and his mother has made it possible for me to reconstruct the extraordinary life history of this Hungarian immigrant who became a Quebec revolutionary.

The outcome of Schirm's coup was, of course, a blow to the prestige of the FLQ. This was certainly not the way to win Quebec over to the cause of independence. Not wanting to concede defeat, the FLQ sent a communiqué dated 1 September, 1964 to all French-Canadian newspapers. Only *Le Devoir* published it (on 3 September), as a curiosity. Here is the text:

> Last Saturday, a revolutionary commando went into action. During the struggle in which the revolutionary forces were opposed to those of the police, two men were killed. We are not bandits nor murderers, as the police forces deceptively accuse us of being. We are men who love our country and who want its people to be freed.
>
> Leslie MacWilliams became a victim of his stupidity. At the beginning of the attack, the chief commando presented himself clearly as a member of the revolutionary movement. The man should have been wise enough not to interfere, but, on the contrary, as a good Anglo-Saxon, he opposed the action of the commando. The latter therefore cut him down as a collaborator. Let this be a lesson to others!
>
> As to Alfred Pinish[*sic*], everybody knows that he was felled by police bullets.
>
> Moreover, each of the partisans carried with him an authorization, identifying him by name and occupation and revealing his affiliation with the revolutionary movement. We demand that they be treated by Canadian justice as prisoners of war, in conformity with Articles 3 and 4 of the Geneva Convention and with Articles 1 and 2 of the regulations of The Hague.

As one can see, this original interpretation of a hold-up plus homicide is strongly reminiscent of the pathos which characterized the writing of the first wave. It must be pointed out that the term "commando" (originally introduced by Schoeters) appears here for the last time in the clandestine literature of the FLQ. Henceforth the word used will be "action group." It is also noteworthy that the term "requisition," used for the hold-ups of the second wave (ALQ), does not occur here and that the slogan "Independence or Death" (and indeed any reference to a patriotic death) has been dropped.

As to the demand to be treated as prisoners of war, this also goes back to Schoeters. It was never a serious proposition. The Geneva Convention does not recognize "soldiers" clad in civilian clothes. They must wear a recognized uniform or, in exceptional cases, at least a clearly visible armband of a kind previously registered with the International Red Cross. Moreover, one does not see what advantage the FLQ would have gained by being recognized as a military formation. Then the "enemy" would have had the right to keep all their members prisoners till after the end of the "hostilities." As to Schirm presenting himself as the chief of a revolutionary movement and the alleged "authorizations," one can only say they were pure fantasy.

In Number 19 of their clandestine journal, the FLQ continued to use wartime phraseology in speaking of the Schirm group and the seven recruits arrested at St. Boniface:

> Twelve revolutionaries have fallen into the hands of the enemy. Twelve soldiers who had sworn to fight for the liberation of their country. Twelve men for whom the love of the country is more important than their personal interests. Twelve patriots who have chosen dignity and honour. As tens of others in prison, they were beaten up by the police against the most elementary principles of humanity."*
> HONOUR TO OUR BROTHERS! LONG LIVE FREE QUEBEC!

---

* I have been told that only Husserault was beaten up by the police in order that they might obtain information from him. But, of course, that is still one too many.

Schirm's Story: A Modern Epic

François Schirm, prisoner no. 4247 at the Federal Penitentiary of St. Vincent de Paul, was born on 21 May, 1932 in Budapest, the capital of Hungary. Despite his German name, his father was Hungarian; an ancestor had come from Germany in 1526 to help defend Hungary against a Turkish invasion. After the campaign he had settled there.

Ferenc (to give him his original name) was an only child. This annoyed him since he was very sociable and would have liked to have brothers and sisters like his friends. His father was a competent carpenter, conscientious, honest, sober, an excellent tradesman and a good provider. He was firm but not hard. Ferenc, who resembles him physically, adored him. His mother, a very religious woman and more given to sentiment, devoted herself to the two men. She was perhaps a bit too possessive, as is natural for a mother who has only one child. In any case, the Schirm family was an honourable middle-class family. They respected God and the law. They attended Mass regularly. They did not believe in class war. And they did everything to bring up their child well.

The boy had no difficulties at school. Had it not been for World War II, he would probably have become a technician or a craftsman.

During World War II, the father, Johann Schirm, fought in the Hungarian army against the Russians. In 1944, the Russians advanced towards Hungary. Budapest was bombed. Johann Schirm decided to send his family to Austria. Mrs. Schirm moved with her son to Amstetten, a small town with a population of 11,000, situated in the Danube Valley, above Vienna. She found a job at an important factory. No place seemed safer. Ferenc became Franz and attended the Bürgerschule (high school) without difficulties. He was a good student; but before the age of 13 he was to be the witness of inhuman atrocities.

Mrs. Rosa Schirm has written to me about the drama that took place at Amstetten in March 1945. The Luftwaffe had practically disappeared from the skies, but Allied pilots had acquired the habit of flying low and terrorizing the population by throwing bombs and machine-gunning the streets. Franz more than once had run home jumping from tree to tree to evade being hit by a bullet or a shell splinter.

On 14 March, 1945, the people of the town, exasperated by these attacks, lynched two American pilots who had been forced to land by parachute, all the while crying, "American bandits! Murderers!" The revenge for this deed was swift and atrocious. On the following day, 15 March, Amstetten was bombarded continuously from 10 a.m. to 4:30 p.m. Franz, running through the park, reached the closest shelter. He knew that his mother was in the main shelter, made of reinforced concrete. Suddenly it was announced on the radio that a large bomb had completely shattered this refuge. Franz had to be restrained by force from leaving his shelter.

Only four people survived in the main shelter. The 145 victims, over half of them the babies of women workers, were brought out after the bombardment and placed side by side on the street. As if by a miracle, Mrs. Schirm was among the survivors. She was suffering from nervous shock and serious injuries. In order to find her, Franz had to walk past the macabre display of the 145 mangled corpses spread out on the pavement.

Mrs. Schirm was disturbed for three months. She remembered nothing. Her son and neighbours told her afterwards what had happened and how strangely she had acted during the weeks following the bombardment. Once, for example, having decided not to eat any more, she locked up the bread. When the boy, exasperated because he had hardly eaten for three days, tried to force the drawer, his mother beat him.

The arrival of the Russians at Amstetten brought new dangers. The Russian soldiers, often drunk, pillaged the houses, looking for wrist watches, jewellery and hard liquor. Everywhere women were raped, regardless of age. Mrs. Schirm and her son had found refuge in a wooden barrack. The floor consisted of boards placed a few feet above the ground and there was a trap door giving access to the space below. One evening a Russian soldier, so drunk that he just managed to keep himself upright, thumped at the door. Franz, still not quite 13 years old, stood behind the door with an axe in his hand, fiercely determined to knock down this representative of the "glorious Red Army," whose body would have been disposed of through the trap door. Luckily the door held fast and the drunken liberator went away cursing.

After the Russian occupation of Vienna, Mrs. Schirm and her boy had to return to Hungary. He was Ferenc once more. Fourteen years old, he had to quit school to help his father support the family.

Two years later, seeing how the regime oppressed the people whose liberator it claimed to be, Mr. Schirm decided to leave his country. This was in 1947 and the border had not yet been fortified with barbed wire, mines and observation towers with Tommy guns — as is the case today. Johann Schirm, who had always admired the Germans for their industriousness and know-how, decided to take his family to Germany. Since they left Hungary "without permission," the Schirms lost not only their property but their nationality as well. They moved to Bavaria, where the father found a job as a carpenter. Soon he became foreman of the workshop. Later he bought a house. His son worked at the same trade. At work they spoke German; at home, Hungarian.

It is surprising to learn that the boy, although strongly built, did not indulge much in sports. On the contrary, he preferred to read. His favourite books were adventure and travel stories. When he had been younger, he had devoured the books of Karl May, the Fenimore Cooper of the Germans. May, who (like Jules Verne) had never set foot outside his country, wrote boys' stories about Red Indians. In his books, which were extremely popular with young Europeans, he described the heroic battle of the natives against their white invaders. Karl May's Redskins are invariably an honest, courageous and proud people, with a highly developed sense of justice and honour. Their white opponents, on the other hand, are cruel and treacherous Englishmen who never keep their word to the Indians. It is an unequal struggle in which injustice triumphs, the efficient weapons of the colonizers have the last word, brutal force crushes the rights of man, and "might becomes right." The young reader, devouring these pathetic stories, could only be won over to the lost cause of the Indians and learn to detest the white imperialists guilty of the genocide of such a noble race.

In contrast to his father, Franz did not like the German manner. He much preferred the mentality of the French who are less pedantic, more imaginative, and more akin to the Hungarian temperament. Moreover, he was eager to travel in search of adventure. When he was 18 years old, he shocked his parents by declaring that he wanted to join the Foreign Legion. This meant that he had to tear himself violently from his mother who pleaded with him not to break her heart. His father tried to dissuade him from his "folly" by rational arguments. It was to no avail, and the young man left. As he was in splendid physical condition and intelligent, he had no difficulty being accepted by the Legion. From then on, he was known as François Schirm.

It is hard to say why he was so attracted by the Foreign Legion. Most of the recruits of the Legion were young people running away from some personal problem. As far as François was concerned, his motive was rather an overpowering romantic urge. In this he resembled Joseph Conrad who, at the age of 17, left Poland to become a sailor — a profession with which he was only acquainted through boys' books of adventure.

Like most of the recruits in the Legion, François, after less than six months, bitterly regretted his decision, but it was too late since the minimum period of service was five years. After the usual training period, which took place in Algeria, François was sent to Vietnam. He fought bravely. He was promoted to the rank of sergeant and soon was at the head of a company of Vietnamese soldiers. However, he fought without conviction, to save his skin more than anything else. He came to the conclusion that this was a colonial war and that the French cause was lost in advance. He liked the

Vietnamese people and appreciated their old culture and good breeding, but he never learned their language.

After the French defeat in Vietnam, he was sent to North Africa as a parachute trainer. He got to know the Sahara, and the war the Algerian National Liberation Front was waging against the colonial French power. Here also, he was not able to refrain from admiring the commitment and courage of the Algerian guerrillas. It was a savage and merciless fight. The two sides, exasperated by a clandestine war which seemed to last indefinitely, became increasingly more guilty of atrocities. In order to extort information from their prisoners, the French used methods of torture copied from the Nazis. Schirm was disgusted by these cruelties; moreover he secretly sided with his enemies. Knowing that here too, the French cause was lost, he left the Foreign Legion after six years of service. He took his leave at Marseilles in 1956, several years before the Algerian war was ended. He was now 24 years old. He could have become a French citizen had he stayed in France. He was still a stateless person and his decision to leave France was possibly the biggest mistake of his life.

During his campaign, François Schirm had corresponded with a young Hungarian girl who lived in Montreal. He had obtained her address through a newspaper. She was a medical secretary. He knew her only through her letters and by her photograph. Many of the Legionaries had similar correspondents who perhaps seemed the more attractive the more distant they were. Schirm decided to go to Canada to acquire a home and a family and to begin a normal way of life. After a short visit to his parents in Bavaria, he crossed the ocean.

He arrived in Montreal in 1957, married the Hungarian girl in 1958, and for the first time since his childhood, had a home. His wife gave birth to a girl. Despite financial problems, which forced his wife to go back to work as a medical secretary, everything might have gone well. He adored his little daughter. Unfortunately, he did not get along with his wife and still less with her mother who lived with them. His spouse was not able to respect a man who earned so little and yet wanted to run the show. They had bought furniture on credit but had difficulty paying the instalments. Ideally, marriage was supposed to provide him with a home and a stability which the adventurer, weary of adventure, had never known; the reality proved otherwise. He felt that his wife and his mother-in-law wanted to dominate him, something he was unable to tolerate. In 1961 they separated and his wife left for the United States, taking the little girl with her. Later he learned that she had divorced him in Reno and had married an American doctor. All that remains for him is a photograph of his little daughter Sylvia, a photograph which he cherishes more than any other worldly possession.

Schirm was no more successful in his work than he was in his marriage. Despite an above-average intelligence, he had never learned a trade. Service in the Foreign Legion was a poor preparation for civilian life. It is true that he had become a man who seemed to fear nothing. He was used to severe discipline and he could be completely trusted. He did not drink or smoke. He had never had the least trouble with the law. Besides speaking French fluently, he also spoke English. He still knew Hungarian and German — bringing his languages up to four.

In Montreal, his experiences were similar to those of many immigrants: no one seemed to need him. He had to be content to work as a bricklayer and later as a glazier. He was forced to quit the latter job because of a work accident. As he was cutting a glass pane, a small splinter pierced his left arm. The wound healed and closed itself but the piece of glass, shaped like a minute dagger, travelled along the forearm with the muscular contractions and cut a nerve. Finally the glass splinter was tracked down and removed. Schirm spent six days in the hospital, during which time he received three-quarters of his salary. The Workmen's Compensation Board refused to make further payments. Yet his left hand, which he could not close, remained weak and incapacitated for a long time. He needed physiotherapy but he got none. Even today he cannot bend his left thumb. During six years of war he had never received such an injury!

Feeling incapable for a time of exacting manual labour, Schirm then found a job as a private agent with the Security Investigation

Company. The company received $2 per hour for his services, of which they paid him $1.05. On top of that they made deductions for his uniform! He felt humiliated and exploited. S.I.C. first sent him to Brinks Express Company. Armed with a revolver, he travelled around the city and throughout the province guarding millions of dollars. Brinks probably never had a better guard — and at such a bargain price! Then the S.I.C. placed him with Steinberg Limited, where he was employed as night watchman at the Miracle Mart of Pont Viau, a suburb of Montreal. There he worked between seventy and eighty hours a week, still at $1.05 per hour. To improve his situation, he took a Diesel mechanics course at a private institute. He worked hard and obtained a worthless degree.

At the Miracle Mart François had come to know a night cleaner, Gilles, a French Canadian who, from the point of view of education and intelligence did not come up to Schirm, though, he was earning $1.55 an hour. The two men became friends and often discussed Quebec's political problems. François continued to be an excellent watchman and a man ready to brave all danger. It is disturbing to think that this man, who would never have betrayed his employer's confidence, later conspired to commit armed robbery elsewhere.

At the time of his arrival in Canada, Schirm had been ignorant of Quebec's history and its political and social problems. He had absolutely nothing against "les Anglophones" — the English-speaking Canadians. This attitude was to change as a result of his humiliating experiences in the working world, however. He had proven himself in the Foreign Legion, but in Canada he was treated as a man with no experience — by employers who were English. He earned less than his wife! Often he lacked the money to pay for a sandwich or a coke!

On top of everything, the federal government also did its part to alienate Schirm from the "English." In 1963 he applied for Canadian citizenship. On the application form he omitted to mention that he had spent four months in Florida, in the summer of 1962. Discovering this, the federal bureaucracy decided to postpone his application for two years. It was a hard blow for a man without a country. Two years later, Schirm was in prison. He may never obtain Canadian citizenship. On the other hand, no other country is obliged to accept him. He could easily live until the year 2000 or longer, and if he stays in prison until the end of his life this "foreigner," no matter how intelligent, strong and capable of working, will have cost the Canadian government the round sum of $200,000, interest included.

Feeling himself treated as a third-class citizen by the ruling English class (the Québecois being second-class citizens), he identified himself more and more with the underprivileged and with all those who considered themselves victims of Anglo-Saxon exploitation. He first became a member of the Rassemblement pour l'indépendance nationale (RIN), and was very active there for some time. But soon he decided that this movement was not revolutionary enough. Schirm belongs to those who believe in the "all or nothing" principle. When he learned about the existence of the Front de libération québecois (FLQ), he identified himself with it. During April and May of 1963, when the first bombs exploded in Montreal and in Westmount mail boxes, François Schirm saw the dawn of the revolution. "That's it," he exclaimed; "it's starting." The soldier spirit in him reawakened. By nature deeply romantic and incapable of realizing his dreams in marriage or in travel, he came to believe in armed revolution as the sole way of liberating man. He was thirsty for action. What would happen afterwards hardly interested him.

Travelling through the bush and practically virgin forests of Quebec, he exclaimed, "What ideal country for underground war! Here is the perfect bushland for partisans! Nobody could hunt out the revolutionaries here!" It seems that Schirm forgot two things: the harshness of the Canadian winter (which he hoped to brave by borrowing a house north of Quebec City), and the fact that a revolutionary army could not subsist without the support, voluntary or enforced, of the local population. And it was highly unlikely that the Quebec farmers, naturally opposed to the idea of a revolution, would go along with this wildly romantic enterprise.

A training camp for the future ARQ was established. Schirm was the soul of this odd army. The recruits wore the letters ARQ on a blue badge. But there were not enough arms. The armed robbery at International Firearms was to provide him with fifty to one hundred rifles and ammunition, as well as with a sum of several thousand dollars, enough to "get into high gear." Gilles knew the rifle store because he had sometimes bought hunting ammunition there.

The fatal outcome of the hold-up, during which five of the accomplices were arrested, put an end to the underground campaign. The training camp was invaded by the police. The revolutionary army (seven youths, the others having fled) was arrested. They spent ten weeks in jail, after which they were released.

Despite his intelligence, François Schirm showed a fantastic lack of judgement. How could he imagine that a badly trained "army" of a dozen, even of a hundred young enthusiasts could become a serious danger to the "system"? What is more, the people with whom he worked did not exactly have the necessary qualities for staging an armed uprising. Even among his four immediate subordinates, at least two showed a lack of nerve. A third, Edmond, lost his head during the hold-up. It does not take much courage to paint the letters FLQ on walls under the cover of night. How would these people act in face of real danger? The hold-up gave a partial reply to this question, a reply that was anything but reassuring.

Schirm also knew, as we all do, that the young of today are used to comfort and do not wish to suffer deprivation. Never having experienced hunger, thirst, or dangerous exposure, but used to beds, heated houses and running hot and cold water, these young people would have found it very difficult to fight long under primitive conditions. However, Schirm seemed confident in his youths. After all, in the Legion he had seen young men from Germany, Belgium, Switzerland and Holland, sometimes from well-to-do families, become hardened soldiers. He expected to see the same phenomenon at the St. Boniface camp — a hard life, rigorous discipline and military training overcoming North American softness.

François is very European, very Hungarian. His remotest forefather had defended (although unsuccessfully) Hungary against the invasion of Soliman the Turk. Due to his education and heritage,

François always kept a Hungarian sense of pride. Patriotism, for him, is to be proud of one's country, to exalt it.

François Schirm is, above all, a military man and not an ideologist. As is the case with most military men (Eisenhower, for example), the question of what is going to happen after the "victory" does not worry him.

Schirm has been in prison since 29 August, 1964. First he was condemned "to be hanged by [his] neck till death ensues." He appealed this sentence and was given a new trial on 10 October, 1967, after which he was sentenced to life imprisonment for non-capital murder. During his stay at Bordeaux prison, he once almost succeeded in escaping. He served time at St. Vincent de Paul penitentiary until 8 May, 1969, when he was transferred to Cowansville.

On 21 May, 1969, Schirm received two letters for his 37th birthday. The first was from his mother; the second from me. In my letter I expressed my best wishes for his birthday and I added, "Speaking statistically, you now have the first half of your life behind you. What are you going to do with the second half?" On 23 May I had the opportunity of seeing him at Cowansville where I was working on a research project. He thanked me for my letter and I asked him if he had thought about my question. I have rarely been so taken aback and disappointed as when I heard him say, with a smile: "I'll continue just as before." I was thunderstruck. Here was a man who, having voluntarily alienated himself from his family and from our society, a man who had practically wasted his life, seemed not to regret anything. I could but keep quiet.

On 9 June, 1969, I heard on television that Schirm had escaped from the Cowansville institution but had been recaptured. I was infuriated for two reasons: first, because Schirm had abused the confidence that the authorities had placed in him; and secondly because the English speaker, true to English linguistic ignorance, deformed a sound Continental name by making it rhyme with "squirm." A few days later, I saw Schirm (Sheerm) again. He seemed to be proud of his exploit, like a schoolboy who had played a trick on his teacher. He also explained to me that a ladder had been placed near the prison wall shortly before the escape.

François Schirm is still a revolutionary. He may sign some of his letters "revolutionarily yours." He may even write them in red ink! He does not regret anything except the fact that two innocent people were killed during the hold-up. He never wanted to kill anyone. He was the only one who had remained calm. As soon as someone was killed, he knew that the cause was lost and that they had to get out. He had never staged a hold-up before but had learned the procedure from an FLQ pamphlet.

Prison has hardened him even more. "Either you are broken or else you become still more revolutionary," he declares. He refuses to be broken.

On 1 January, 1969, his father died in Germany, after an illness lasting four years. He never knew that his son was in prison. Schirm has inherited three-eighths of the estate. His mother still lives at Ettenbeuren, Bavaria. He hardly ever writes her.

What about the other prison inmates? François does not identify himself with them. Above all, not with the hold-up men. He does not see himself as a criminal. He would never have stolen a penny for himself. His sense of honour has been deeply hurt by the fact that he is being treated like a common criminal. At war he did not enjoy killing other people and after six years he had had enough of it. He had left the army and wanted to lead an honest life — but without being exploited. . . .

François Schirm is rigid. Like all Hungarians, he hates communism. He is an affable man who gets along well with everybody. He is not a dreamer. He does not decorate his cell with pictures of half-nude women. In everyday life, he is flexible and realistic. But he is also, perhaps incurably, a romantic.

If the revolution of Quebec does not succeed, he will remain a criminal in the eyes of society. He may never become a guard, for example, despite his basic integrity. He may remain a man without a country — indeed, an undesirable. It will be difficult for him to get a job in which he will not be exploited. And the vicious circle will recommence. He has no friends in Canada, no visitors, no correspondence except from his mother! He has hardly any friends. He will probably never see his mother again who has been crying and praying for him for years. Will he ever see his daughter?

The Hungarians have always been a proud people. In this respect, Schirm is very Hungarian. His "revolutionary" pride is the only thing he can cling to, the only thing that keeps him on his two feet and protects him against the humiliation of seeing himself as a failure. Today he is still too proud to admit his faults and to make peace with society. Nothing could better characterize the tragedy of this capable man than the verse which Dante addresses to a prisoner in hell: "The fact that your pride has never been broken constitutes your greatest punishment."*

* *Divine Comedy,* Song XIV.

The Schirm Group

The Schirm group of terrorists consisted of six persons, not counting the dozen recruits of the training camp. Apart from the 32-year-old chief, there were Cyr, 26; Edmond, 20; Gilles, 28; Marc-André, 20; and Marcel, 22. Marc-André P. did not take part in the hold-up. He was the leader and cook of the training camp in the absence of Schirm. During the hold-up, he may have been waiting nearby with another car. He was arrested on 1 September, but was released six weeks later for lack of evidence.

With the exception of Schirm, all members of the group were French Canadians. There was no intellectual among them. Three were sons of workers, one had grown up on a small farm. Only one had learned a trade. Two were unemployed at the time. Edmond was the only full-time militant of the FLQ.

Three of these partisans were much older than the members of preceding FLQ's. Edmond, 20, who had fired the fatal shot, was the youngest and the most indoctrinated. Before, he had been transporting dynamite from one place to another. None of the members had a code name and none possessed any means of identification. The group was far from homogenous, since two of the members, Cyr and Marcel, had only just been won over by Marc-André with whom they shared an apartment. As to Gilles, he was against the use of weapons from the very beginning. Nor were they on the same wave-length ideologically. Schirm was strongly anti-communist, Edmond believed in Marxism and class war, Gilles and Marcel had no political convictions whatsoever, still less ideological training. They simply wanted to further the cause of independence, but without socialism. All members, except Schirm, came from families with a great number of children. Two of them had been serving in the

Canadian Armed Forces and had undergone all the humiliations which were normally inflicted upon French Canadians by their English-speaking comrades.

The following biographical details may be of interest to the reader:

1. Edmond the Doctrinaire

This young man had just reached the age of 21 when the judge read him the following sentence:

The sentence now pronounced against you, Edmond . . . is that you be returned to the prison of the district whence you came and that, on Friday, 22 October of this year, within the precincts of the prison where you will be held, you be hanged by the neck till death ensues. May God have mercy on your soul!

This verdict, read solemnly by Judge André Sabourin on 21 May, 1965 at 9:30 p.m. before the Court of Sessions of Montreal, was not carried out. When the date of the hanging approached, Judge Sabourin died suddenly of a heart attack, while Edmond got a reprieve of six months. He was kept on death row. The date of the execution was postponed to 22 April, 1966, then again postponed to 30 September, 1966, then to 25 September, 1967. Then a new date was set: 3 November, 1967, followed by another postponement to 29 March, 1968. Again, one day before the execution, a telegram announced another postponement. Finally, on 15 October, 1968, the cat ceased to play with the mouse. Edmond had a new trial and this time was condemned, for capital murder, to life imprisonment. The Canadian Parliament had abolished the death penalty.

Already, during and after the first trial, Edmond's truly tragic case made a deep impression. Edmond was defended by Maître Juteau, who gave his services free. Edmond had handed him a detailed biography. Andrée Benoist, a lady psychologist, also came to the rescue. She wrote a psychological and sociological report for the judge, who refused to accept it. The report was published in *Parti Pris*, and later in the book *Les Québecois* (Maspéro, Paris, 1967), under the title "Le dossier Schirm-Guénette" ("The Schirm-Guénette File"). It is most revealing.

The psychologist declared that Edmond had gone through traumatizing experiences during his childhood and youth, that he had been obliged to quit school in order to assist his father financially, and that he had worked for Northern Electric where the work was in English only. He had discovered great poverty in Montreal and had been disappointed with the many politicians who promise much and keep little. The FLQ seemed to offer the most radical way to do something about this state of affairs.

Mrs. Benoist wrote that Edmond belonged to the adolescent sub-culture which "nowadays, reaches from age ten to twenty and beyond." Adolescence is characterized by insecurity, the need to discover one's identity, the need of an ideal, and thirst for justice. The ideology of the FLQ "fulfils the old adolescent dream of a new society" where justice and liberty reign, allowing man to develop fully. In this group not only Edmond but many others had found a means to express their identity. The present social problems automatically produce these ideological groups "who want to reform the adult world by every means." Edmond's behaviour had to be judged within this context.

The death sentence had its repercussions in France also. Sixty French-Canadian students living in Paris sent a protest note to the Canadian Ambassador in Paris, His Excellency Jules Léger. A great number of well-known French personalities, among them two members of the Académie Française, submitted a plea for clemency to the Prime Ministers of both Canada and Quebec.

Who was Edmond?

Edmond was the youngest of the five men involved in the hold-up. Only four months before that fatal event he had left the home of his parents in order to be free. Here was a young man thirsty for liberty who had taken the life of a man, aged 56, who had dared to act as a free man. In one second an idealist had become a murderer. His father, a retired worker, who knew nothing of the clandestine activities of his son, heard the news the same evening on TV and was profoundly shocked. He fell ill and has never been well since.

Crime follows its own laws. Those who use criminal methods, even if only temporarily and for a "cause," are no longer their own masters. The law of crime dictates that resistance on the part of the victim must be crushed at all costs, even at the price of his life. After which the offender does absolutely nothing to assist the victim — who is now considered as the real culprit. Without being an authentic criminal, Edmond instinctively followed the laws of criminal behaviour. When the police arrived, he hailed a nearby taxi and forced the driver, under threat of his rifle, to drive him to Rosemount, thus robbing a poor man of $2.

Edmond is the only delinquent in his family. He has two brothers who are factory workers and married. They seem to be quite satisfied with their condition. Edmond has also five sisters, of whom three are married. Three more sisters died as children. Edmond was the ninth of eleven children. His father worked in a factory and in a store on weekends in order to support his large family. In fact, Edmond never lacked anything. The father was not a man given to revolt, though he was a convinced unionist who disliked the "American" unions.

Edmond lost his mother when he was 3 years old. He does not remember her at all. He was soon placed, together with two of his siblings, in an orphanage near Montreal. The institution was run by nuns who, Edmond says, were without feelings. But there were also a number of unwed mothers working in the orphanage, and of these Edmond has the best of memories. They liked the children and it is probable that they needed the affection of the children in return.

Edmond's father remarried after some years but Edmond had to stay in institutions until he was 10, when he was allowed to go home. There he found a strange woman whom he distrusted, and two little half-brothers. Edmond could never get along with his second mother, nor with his half-brothers who seemed to have more rights than the children of the first marriage. This created considerable tension in the family, and Edmond's brothers left home very young without finishing their schooling. They were therefore unable to learn a trade. Edmond stayed at home much longer than his brothers, because he wanted to finish his schooling and also because he got along very well with his father. However, after completing grade ten, he left school in order to make a living. He would have liked to continue his studies, but did not want to live at the expense of his father. He found a job with Northern Electric where, owing to his intelligence, he soon became a microfilm photographer. He began with a salary of $25 weekly, was promoted, and soon got $75.

Once on his own, Edmond ran into a love problem, then into political problems. In June 1964, he decided to drop his job and work full-time for the FLQ. He soon came to know Schirm who was, in a way, the prototype of a freedom fighter. After less than three months of clandestine work, Edmond found himself in prison on a charge of capital murder.

Edmond was strongly influenced by the fact that an uncle, Georges Guénette, 24, had been killed by two RCMP officers on 7 May, 1944 (the year Edmond was born). The uncle had been violently against conscription and, with five others, had beaten up a policeman so badly that the man became a mental patient for the rest of his life. When the officers had come to arrest Georges he fled across a field, and had been shot. The affair caused a sensation and remained vivid in the family memory.

Edmond had more intellectual interests than the rest of the family. He liked and respected his father very much, and his father was proud of him. Edmond loved to read modern authors, French or American. He read Camus (*The Rebel* and other works), Faulkner and Hemingway; liked to discuss social and political questions; to play chess; and to go swimming. He loved to listen to the songs of the French-Canadian "chansonniers," songs that often had political undertones. When the crime cut through his life, he was in full development, both intellectually and emotionally.

Edmond has been in prison since September 1964. During this time he has never been inactive, nor demoralized. But the atmosphere of a prison is not an atmosphere where a young man can develop normally. Most of the decisions are made for him, not by him. In the eyes of the world, he is a criminal, and that is difficult to take. He lives very much by himself, does not talk to the guards, and talks little to other inmates except those belonging to the FLQ. He is one of those political criminals who become more of a doctrinaire in prison, perhaps as a form of self-defence against feelings of guilt. Edmond considers himself a victim of certain circumstances, but he overlooks the fact that he put himself into a situation where a tragic accident could happen, especially as he had brought a loaded gun with him. Edmond has not yet come to terms with his crime. His excuses — "I was very young," "MacWilliams should not have resisted" — sound weak even in his own ears. Of course, the first wave used those stock excuses of all "revolutionaries": "No revolution without bloodshed; that's the price we (!) have to pay for a better society," etc., but a strong individual like Edmond will never be satisfied with stock phrases. Nor does he have a romantic-mystic conception of violence as "the ritual of the new religion."

It must be said that the general climate of violence reigning in Montreal blunts the awareness of many young people as to the consequences of criminal acts. Moreover they tend to view the resistance of a victim as a provocation, if not as a downright attack.

Edmond's political convictions are very simple. He believes in the ideas of Pierre Vallières concerning the "liberation" of man. He makes one think of those young people who believe that once they are independent of their parents all problems will be solved. Edmond tends to see everything in black and white. Kept in the artificial world of a penitentiary, he has time to think, but no opportunity to apply his thoughts to reality. He is very sure of himself. He is one of those young people who believe they have all the answers. This is natural at his age. But does one have the right to impose one's answers upon others at gun point?

The three biographies which follow have also been written with the collaboration of the individuals concerned who gave permission to publish, on condition that their real names be withheld.

2. *Alex, Revolutionary with Mental Reservations*

Born in October 1937, Alex was one of ten children. He grew up on a small farm. With the exception of the youngest girl, all his siblings are adults and doing well. The family was united. Alex respected his parents very much. Alcoholism and delinquency were unknown. At the age of 17, Alex finished grade ten. He could have continued to study but, wanting to become independent, he enrolled in the Armed Forces where he learned the trade of electric technician. He also took a course as a mechanic. For the three years preceding his arrest he worked as a technician for a Canadian Army base. His salary was $4,200 per year.

Alex had always been a great reader who spent a lot of money for books. Intending to marry, he would have liked to be promoted and get a better pay. However, he found it difficult to master the English language and thus had no chance of promotion. This made him bitter. He felt that Quebec was too dependent on the Anglo-Saxons who, in his place of work, occupied all the higher posts. He became interested in politics and was attracted by separatist movements which promised to put the French Canadian in his rightful place. To a degree he adopted Marxism, feeling that there was a class war between the dominating English and the French working class with which he identified himself. He even read the *Thoughts of Mao*. On the other hand, he was quite bourgeois in his tastes: he wanted to marry his fiancée, buy a home, etc.

Alex has thought a great deal about politics. He cannot accept his life sentence. He wrote to the parole board the following lines which I quote with his permission: "By nature I am neither a criminal nor a thief. I acted according to my conscience. I made a mistake. I have learned that violence does not lead anywhere. Personally, I have never used violence. I am against violence. But I am all for social justice and want to work for it."

Alex has always been a good worker and a good student. He has never wasted his time, not even in prison. While in jail, under the most unfavourable conditions, he completed grades eleven and twelve with an average of 82%. After this he was placed in the kitchen — the only strenuous work in the penitentiary (seven days a week, from morning till evening). Since autumn 1969, he has been taking a course as IBM programmer, and in 1970 finished at the top of the class. He has taken correspondence courses in the economic geography of Canada, radio, electricity, bookkeeping, automobile mechanics. He has not had any holiday for six years.

He was introduced to the FLQ by Marc-André P., whose apartment he shared at the time. He accepted the aims of the FLQ without approving of its methods. Like Edmond, he is of small body build, a fact which may contribute to his sense of ambition. He does not smoke, never drank, and never thought of using drugs. He is a quiet, peaceful man whose only link with the FLQ now is the fact that he is being incarcerated with a number of other members. This is a young man who will certainly find his way in life — if Ottawa allows him to leave the penitentiary. He has a job lined up for him with a monthly salary of $625 and is waiting to be freed on parole.

Alex is more realistic and more sober in his thinking than most ex-terrorists. Having never been spoilt in his life, he can accept the inevitable. Like most young people who think, he is all for social justice. He doubts whether it is compatible with capitalism and materialism, but he has learned that social justice cannot be realized by force. During his years of "doing time" in a penitentiary, he has matured a great deal. He never has been a doctrinaire and never will be.

3. Roch the Soldier

Edmond, as we have seen, came from a difficult family. His friend Roch passed through childhood experiences which he describes as "hell." Conditions at home were such that all the children left as early as possible. One of his half-brothers ran away at the early age of 12, never to return.

Roch was born in May 1942 in an industrial town near Lake St. Jean. His father worked for ALCAN Aluminium Company. Roch stresses the fact that the company paid his father well. The trouble in the family came from another source. His father had lost his first wife, leaving him with five girls and two boys. He married again and had two more boys, of which Roch was the first. The children of the first marriage did not accept their stepmother and there were constant quarrels and beatings. Roch was not spared either. He says that he was often whipped by his mother and that the father was too weak to interfere. It seems that his mother hated the children of the first marriage, but that she also rejected her son Roch, while spoiling the youngest. Because of his parents' behaviour, the boy lost all faith in religion at an early age. He could not accept a religion which, he thought, told children to honour their parents without saying anything about the respect due to a child.

When he was growing up, Roch had two friends, both intelligent. One came from an united family, did well in school and later got on well in life. He does not believe in separatism, but in competing with the English on equal terms. Roch and the other friend (Marc-André P.) came from unfavourable home conditions, did badly at school, became sailors, and wound up with the FLQ. One has the feeling that they made society responsible for their failure.

Roch says that the constant tension at home prevented him from doing his homework and from concentrating at school. He repeated several classes and finally quit school at 17, having reached only grade seven. He then enrolled in the Royal Canadian Navy. He had always been attracted by the military. When only 4 or 5 years old, he had worn a coat made of military cloth and played at war with his young uncle. At that time there was a military camp nearby, complete with a brass band. When the band played, Roch marched to the tune like a soldier. Nothing made him happier. He wanted to become a soldier and go off to war. But in 1959 there was no war and he had to be satisfied with the navy. He served there from the end of 1959 to August 1963. During this time, he took a course in electricity and began training as a torpedo-launcher.

We have already mentioned the singular satisfaction Roch felt when wearing a uniform. Obviously the uniform gave him a feeling of virility and prestige. Moreover, whenever he discharged a piece, a rifle, cannon or torpedo, or whenever he heard the boom of an explosion, he experienced a singular sensation of liberation and valour. This went back to his childhood when the sound of drums had given him the same satisfaction. As a boy of about 10, he had discovered a jar belonging to his mother which contained rouge powder. When he blew into the powder, a wonderful rosy cloud formed in the air — as after an explosion. When he was about 15, his mother bought a little machine to mark the hemline of dresses.

It consisted of an adjustable stand which allowed one to project some white powder on the garment by pressing a rubber ball. He played with this marker because the white jets of powder reminded him of the smoke forming after the discharge of a cannon. When he was in the navy, he loved to use a machine filled with pesticide. By activating a lever, a jet of white liquid was projected into the crevices of the floor, killing the beetles hiding there. During commando exercises, he also experienced a feeling of power, especially when transporting explosives on his back or when hearing the sound of explosions.

It is clear that Roch was fascinated — "liberated" — by violence of a certain kind. It gave him a feeling of superiority which momentarily compensated for the profound feelings of inadequacy and inferiority which had been implanted into him during his childhood and adolescence. Since he had been virtually emasculated at home, the rifle and cannon shots, the explosions, the torpedo shots became for him the symbols of a virility which had to assert itself strongly in order to keep the upper hand. The clouds of rosy powder, the jets of white powder, and of pesticide of course had the same meaning. One understands now why Roch was so attracted by the military and finally by the revolutionary army of the FLQ.

During his service in the navy, Roch proudly wore the Canadian uniform with the letters HMCS (Her Majesty's Canadian Ship). When in a port of a French colony, he naturally spoke French, to the great astonishment of everyone. How could a sailor in the service of Her Majesty speak French? This question annoyed him every time, but what irritated him much more was the treatment he got from the crew who were overwhelmingly English-speaking. Again and again they humiliated him by deriding his French, by calling him "a pea souper," or by alluding to his French temperament by naming him "a frog." When he spoke French with one of the few French Canadians on board, his English-speaking comrades would become hostile and ridicule him.

In August 1963, Roch fell into a depression of some kind. He was hospitalized for about six months. Then he learned that he was discharged from the navy for good, a fact which again kindled his inferiority complex. Without uniform and without arms, he felt a nobody. It is true that the Queen put $2,500 in his pocket when he left the hospital, but what does a sailor do with so much money? He wasted it in night clubs, on women, buying drinks for others, etc. He planned to become a sailor on the Great Lakes, following the example of his friend Marc-André P., but the plan fell through. He finally went home, did nothing, and had to leave when the rest of his money was almost gone.

During his travels with the navy, Roch had corresponded with a young woman living in his home town. With $2,500 in his pocket, he could have married her. Seeing that he did nothing of the kind, however, his fiancée threw him over and married someone else. The dismissal from the navy "for reasons of health" was a second defeat. Roch did not feel accepted at home, nor by the neighbourhood, but he was accepted by his schoolmate Marc-André P., who took him into his apartment in Montreal and introduced him to the FLQ. Roch visited the training camp of St. Boniface. The military atmosphere and the uniform fascinated him; the two weeks spent in that camp were among the happiest days of his life. He left the camp in order to play his part in the hold-up of International Firearms, was arrested and sentenced to life imprisonment for non-capital murder. Once more, when trying to assert himself as a man, he found himself precipitated to the very bottom of the ladder.

Roch says he did not so much believe in independence as in the necessity for giving the French language its rightful place. He is still an intelligent man who writes more correct French than the prison guards who order him around. The contempt for the French language in the navy left a deep impression, especially as it seemed also to be a contempt for his person as a French Canadian. He was not only attracted to the FLQ because of the military atmosphere, but also because he hoped that the actions of the FLQ would help to save the French language from the onslaught of the English.

Freud would have had no difficulty discovering an inferiority complex in Roch. Adler would have considered him a classical example of a man suffering from feelings of inadequacy and trying to overcompensate for them. And Jung would have pointed out that

Roch, having lost the traditional religious faith very early, was very much in need of another idol and a new faith in order to live meaningfully. Moreover, not having had a proper father figure in his youth, he found such a figure in the person of Schirm the freedom fighter. And the new society which the FLQ promised to establish would at last be that paternal home where all the children had the same rights, the same security, and the same recognition. Roch's tragedy is that, instead of achieving his goal, he has found himself placed — and in the name of the Queen too — in a federal penitentiary where the rights are as scarce as they were at home and where he stays in a badly lit cell twenty-four hours a day. He no longer believes in violence.

Military service over the years is a bad preparation for civil life. Roch was never able to work after his discharge from the navy. (His younger brother, by the way, is also unable to earn a living and has been admitted several times to a mental hospital.)

In August 1971 (!) Roch will at last be eligible for parole. He says he cannot imagine lasting that long. Moreover, Ottawa may refuse to parole him. . . .

4. *"They won't catch me again"*

Xavier was the fifth of seven children. His father, who had worked as a mechanic in a factory for thirty years, retired in 1968. The family life was sound. There was no alcoholism, no delinquency in the family as far back as one could remember. Xavier had two brothers who became qualified workers. They are both married with children, as are his four sisters. In short, it was a typical French-Canadian family, living modestly, but satisfied.

Xavier was born in November 1935. He remembers that during the wartime years the family lived in a suburb, had a vegetable garden and a few hens. Unlike his siblings, Xavier found learning difficult. Quite intelligent in all practical pursuits, he was not gifted intellectually. In his own words: "Nothing entered my head." He only reached grade six, whereas his brothers left school after grade eight and grade eleven, respectively. This naturally gave Xavier a feeling of inferiority. As a 16-year-old he began to work as a delivery boy for a grocery. A year later, he worked in a dairy for another twelve months, and then became a cleaner at the University of Montreal. Three years later he worked as a painter in a steel firm. He left there to work as driver of a delivery van and finally took a job as a cleaner in another firm.

He married at 19, and his wife was the same age. The marriage was quite happy. They had three boys and two girls. Everything would have been well had Xavier not walked into what he calls "the trap of the FLQ." He too resented that the English seemed to have the best jobs everywhere (His bosses were English-speaking), and he was in favour of separatism, though not of socialism.

Xavier was extremely humiliated by his incarceration. He felt that Schirm had exploited his readiness to render service. He asked his wife to forget him but she came regularly to visit him in the penitentiary. Life was exceedingly hard for her. Alone, she could not cope with five children. She had to live in a real slum. (I have visited her.) She first received a "needy mother" allowance of $145 per month, later of $175, which was not enough to feed and clothe the family after the monthly rent of $80 had been paid. She struggled for five years, then the Social Welfare had to place the children elsewhere, at much higher expense.

I had a number of talks with Xavier, asking him how a man so honest could go along with such a criminal scheme. He had good moral values and had never been an extremist or a rebel. The way he was brought up had taught him to be satisfied with a modest income. He had his pleasures too; he loved to go camping in the summer time.

It seems that Schirm made a great impression on Xavier, especially when he told him some war anecdotes. One story told by Schirm was as impressive as it was untrue: Schirm said that when he was thirteen years old and living in a barrack with his parents, the Russians had entered and shot both his father and his mother, leaving him, a scared orphan, behind.

Schirm also introduced him to the training camp at St. Boniface. Xavier saw only a few tents there and some would-be guerrillas. He was told these people were trained to take part in political demonstrations against the war in Vietnam or in connection with strikes. Then Schirm took him to the meeting on Davidson Avenue and assigned him his role in the hold-up.

After his arrest, he broke all solidarity with the hold-up group. Of all the militants of the FLQ I have known, he was the only one to be deeply ashamed at what he had done.

In the penitentiary, Xavier showed great maturity and fortitude. Everybody respected him. Rather introverted, he was extremely preoccupied by the fate of his family. He worked in the kitchen, the most strenuous work in the penitentiary, and had the reputation of being a very reliable person.

Xavier cannot say for sure what the real plans of Schirm were. Apparently he was rather left in the dark. He certainly never dreamed of battles!

During 1969, great efforts were made by the officials of the penitentiary, the classification officer, the psychologist and myself to obtain parole for this really pathetic case. Xavier was then 34 years old, had a job assured and was urgently needed at home both as a provider and as head of the family. He had done five years of his term. Considering that the leaders of the first wave (with two victims) had been paroled after three years, everybody expected the Parole Board in Ottawa to be clement. To the dismay of everyone, the answer from Ottawa was a resounding NO. The Parole Board consists of a number of English-speaking functionaries. Those who pleaded for parole, including Xavier himself, were French Canadians. Once more it seemed that the English wanted to show their power and their superiority over the French. From the psychological as well as the personal point of view, the decision was deplorable. It was finally corrected in March 1970, when the Parole Board reversed its decision, and Xavier now works as a truck driver.

The Schirm hold-up took place in August 1964. One year later, Jean-Marc Piotte, in *Parti Pris* (September 1965), took a rather dim view of the whole enterprise. He wrote that such actions could create "a state of neurosis in the population," but never a revolutionary climate. To believe the opposite was to fall into subjectivism: "If there are guys who need to hear the noise of bombs in order to remain committed, it would be better to dismiss them." After all, the effect of such violent acts is short-lived, because they are motivated by the subjective needs of certain individuals. "To try, by an armed action, to accelerate the historical process, means walking on one's head."

Railway Interlude

August 1965

In their clandestine journal No. 26, dated 1 January, 1965, the FLQ had published detailed and illustrated instructions for "the destruction of a railway track." More instructions followed on 15 April. Then, at the beginning of June, two acts of sabotage derailed two trains. One train was coming from New Brunswick with a cargo of potatoes, the other from Ontario with vegetables. Moreover, a freight train was "attacked" with a Molotov cocktail. The three acts were directed against the Canadian National Railways. They were gleefully reported in the FLQ journal. The explanation was that the FLQ wanted to protest in this way against the importation from "abroad" of agricultural products which Quebec (they thought) was able to produce herself.

During the summer of 1965, Prime Minister Lesage of Quebec made a sort of public relations tour of Western Canada, trying to give an answer to that perennial question: What does Quebec want? During that tour he declared to some students that he was going to put an end to terrorism and separatism in Quebec. ("I will smash them.") Hearing this, three men in Quebec decided to show this "collaborator" and "traitor" that the hydra of terrorism had grown a new head.

On 2 August a bomb explosion damaged the track of the CNR at Ste Madeleine, not far from St. Hyacinthe, shortly before the passage of a passenger train. Thanks to the vigilance of the staff, the train was brought to a stop in time and a possible catastrophe averted.

On the same day, a bomb was found on the CPR railway bridge at Bordeaux near Montreal. Not being provided with a detonator, it was only meant to frighten, not to explode.

One of the instigators of these acts was arrested on 22 August, 1965. He explained that the second bomb had been placed on the CPR bridge just to find out how long it would take the police to discover it. (In fact, the bomb was found by boys three days after it was placed. The bridge serves also as a passage for pedestrians.)

The man arrested was Gaston Collin, a 32-year-old army veteran. Also arrested was Norman Allard, aged 26. The third accomplice, Lionel Chénette, 30, was not arrested until August 1966, one year after the deed. In the meantime, he had "worked for the Revolution."

Both Collin and Chénette had served many years in the Canadian Army. They both profoundly resented the humiliations many French-Canadian soldiers had to experience in the armed forces because of their language. Both spoke English fluently. And both were unmarried.

Gaston came from Gaspesia, a particularly underprivileged region of Quebec. His father, a tradesman, was never really out of work, and the family — parents and eight children — enjoyed a certain security. Gaston lost his mother when he was 18 years old and already serving in the army, but his father still lives in Gaspesia. The family has the best of reputations: no alcoholism, no delinquency. The children were brought up to respect the law. None was spoilt.

Gaston was intelligent. At age 15 he reached the "ceiling" of the local school: grade eight. Being well developed for his age and looking for opportunities, he enrolled in the army. (They believed him when he said he was 17.) Later he explained that his decision was dictated by the desire to learn something, coupled with the lure of adventure. On both counts, he certainly got what he wanted. For twelve years he served under the Canadian flag. He learned telecommunications and electronics, served in the signal corps, was sent to Korea and later to the Congo. But after twelve years of army service, he had had enough.

In the Canadian Armed Forces, everything happens in English, at least it did at that time. The French-Canadian soldier was only accepted insofar as he spoke English. Gaston, being very French Canadian, was often revolted by the "imperialist" anti-French attitude common in the army. He felt he was treated like a "native," and resented the fact that a mastery of English was an absolute pre- requisite for any promotion. When he left the army with the grade of corporal, he was ready to fight against those injustices he had encountered. He read some "revolutionary" tracts coming from Cuba or France and he was drawn into the orbit of the FLQ.

Lionel Chénette had also served long years in the Canadian army. The story of his youth is one of affective deprivation, for he was brought up in institutions. He was more rigid, more fanatic than Gaston. Both found adjustment to civil life difficult after such a long service in the army. Though, thanks to their skills, they found good work, civil life lacked the excitement of army life.

When Gaston Collin was sentenced, on 7 April, 1967, to two years in penitentiary, the judge took into account the fact that the culprit had already been held nineteen months in prison. Gaston had pleaded guilty to charges of illegal possession of explosives and of conspiracy to endanger human life and property. Chénette did likewise but, having been arrested much later, got four years. Allard was liberated for lack of evidence.

In the penitentiary, Gaston found it easy to submit to discipline. He was never arrogant. He read a lot. He had never read Marcuse, preferring the writings of Durkheim and Auguste Comte, two clas- sics of sociology. But what impressed him most was the book *Soul on Ice* by the black militant Eldrige Cleaver.

One year after his sentence he was freed on parole, a condition of which was that he should not leave Canada without permission. Gaston broke his word and went to Cuba. (One wonders how a person who is not allowed to leave the country can get a Canadian passport at all. Shall we ever know?)

In Cuba, Gaston was employed in sugar cane cutting for three months. There he made the acquaintance of Raymond Villeneuve, another Canadian exile who broke his parole. When the sugar cane harvest was finished, Gaston studied in Havana. Like Villeneuve, he was anything but a free man. The government decided where he must live and what he must do. His letters were censored.

There was no future for him in Cuba, and after nine months, he demanded to be allowed to return home. Back in Canada, because of his breach of parole, he had to do one more year of penitentiary. On 18 August, 1969, he was once more in the "Dome" of St. Vincent de Paul penitentiary.

He has told a journalist of *Petit Journal* and myself about his disenchantment with Cuba. Socialism in practice is very different from the slogans on the wall. The salaries of the workers are frozen. Economic necessities and growth are subordinated to rigid political principles which stifle any private initiative. Costly blunders are made. The Russians have too much to say because they support Cuba financially. There is nothing to buy and hardly enough to eat. But there are model schools and a few model industries which are shown to the foreign visitors (including the CBC). Much is done for the young generation, but those over 20 are practically sacrificed. The diversification of agriculture is painfully slow, but the first grapefruit groves are beginning to bear fruit. Industrialization, too, seems very slow. Hence the lack of goods in the stores.

Like Georges Schoeters before him, Collin has become very critical of Castro's Cuba.

Quebec and the Statue of Liberty

February 1965

This episode can only be explained by the intimate relationship between extremist separatism and anti-Americanism. Indeed, the first FLQ members not only made bombs, they also took an active part in every anti-American demonstration. The same thing holds true of the FLQ of 1965-66. In 1963, the demonstrations had to do with the Bomarc atomic missiles to be installed on Canadian soil for the defence of the North American continent. In 1965-66, the demonstrations were directed at the American Consulate and dealt with the war in Vietnam.

On 26 February, 1965, Mademoiselle Michèle Duclos, aged 38, from Montreal, was arrested in New York. She had been transporting dynamite in her car from Montreal to New York with the intention of blowing up the Statue of Liberty. Three Americans, Robert Steel Collier, Walter Augustus Bowe and Khalhel Sultain Sayved, were named as accomplices. They called the Statue "that damned old witch."

On 1 March, three Montreal men were before the court on the charge of stealing the dynamite: Jean Giroux, 20; Raymond Sabourin, 20; and Gilles Legault, 31. Ten days later, another lady, Mademoiselle Michelle Saulnier, aged 30, was also charged with conspiracy in the same plot. She refused to testify at the preliminary hearing of co-accused Raymond Sabourin. Giroux, Sabourin and Legault were imprisoned in Bordeaux awaiting trial.

On Easter Sunday, 18 April, 1965, Gilles Legault hung himself in his prison cell. *La Cognée* promised, "the murderers of Gilles Legault will have to pay." The leading Quebec novelist Hubert Aquin, hailed by *La Cognée* as a member of the FLQ, and at one time arrested in possession of a stolen car and a revolver, devoted two lines to Gilles in his bestseller *Trou de Mémoire* (1968): "Gilles Legault has just committed suicide in his prison cell; it was on an Easter day: Gilles was a patriot, a brother. . . ."

On 11 May, Jean Giroux was convicted in Montreal of stealing and supplying the dynamite for the bomb plot. Much later, on 16 December, 1966, Michèle Saulnier was acquitted in Montreal of charges arising out of the bomb plot.

Miss Duclos was a militant member of the RIN. She also had been in Algeria in 1963, soon after the country obtained independence. As her friends testified, she always was on the side of the poor and wanted to help them. This is why, when she received the visit of two blacks from New York, on 30 January, 1965, she was easily taken in. R. S. Collier presented himself as the leader of a Black Liberation Front, his friend Ray Woodall as his right-hand man. Their plan was to attract the attention of the world to the plight of the black population in the USA by blowing up the Statue and two other symbols of liberty.

Two weeks later, Miss Duclos left Montreal for New York in her white Rambler. Resting in the luggage compartment was a parcel containing twenty-one sticks of dynamite and three detonators. When she approached New York, she had the impression that she was being followed. She therefore placed her car in a parking lot in the Bronx.

The following morning, Collier and Woodall, accompanied by two other blacks (W. A. Bowes, a judo master, and K. S. Sayved, a student), went to the parking lot in order to retrieve the parcel. When they took it out they were surrounded by a number of policemen and arrested. But Ray Woodall was freed almost immediately: he had acted as undercover agent and informer. His real name was Raymond Wood. Soon afterwards, Michèle Duclos was arrested in a hotel on 31st Street in Manhattan, where she was staying. On 4 March, she pleaded not guilty. Three months later, she pleaded guilty to a charge of smuggling explosives into the USA with the intention of blowing up the Statue. On 18 June, 1965, she was sentenced to five years in penitentiary. However, she was freed and deported to Canada late in September of the same year.

Miss Duclos was a talented musician and a popular speaker on Télé-Métropole (Channel 10) in Montreal. Her father, Major Duclos of the Mount Royal Fusiliers in Montreal, had distinguished himself during the commando raid on Dieppe, in 1942. There is no doubt that Miss Duclos was motivated by the most sincere desire to help, but like so many terrorists used methods which would almost certainly backfire. The twenty-one sticks of dynamite would not have been sufficient to blow up the Statue of Liberty, let alone the Washington Obelisk. The idea actually was to blow up the Statue's arm holding up the torch, and the top of the Washington monument. Both bombs were supposed to explode during the night, when nobody could be hurt.

According to *La Cognée*, the action was not in line with FLQ policy ("You cannot export a revolution"), but the whole procedure and the symbolism of the scheme were obviously modelled on terrorist events in Quebec. As we have seen, the FLQ identified itself, if only after the fact, with Gilles Legault, the first "patriot" to lose his life in connection with a bombing attempt.

Michèle Duclos later went back to Algeria.

The Vallières-Gagnon Group

Fourth Wave, August 1965 to July 1966

This new wave of violence began with the theft of dynamite at Varennes, on the south shore of the St. Lawrence River. The explosives were used to blow up the sender of the English radio station CKTS in Sherbrooke, Quebec (August 1965).

At about the same time, the FLQ organized an information service on the following items: How to commit sabotage, How to steal dynamite, How to hold up a bank, How to make a bomb, How to set a fire etc. — a regular school of crime! The information service was publicized in the clandestine journal *La Cognée,* which came out regularly twice a month at that time.

On 23 October, 1965, members of the group broke into the offices of the New Democratic Party at 3920 St. Hubert Street, Montreal. They stole a Gestetner mimeographic machine and a lot of office material, to be used for their clandestine journal. It was said that the number of copies reached about two hundred at that time. They were distributed from hand to hand to suitable contacts.

At the beginning of November 1965, *La Cognée* published its 46th number. With this issue there was an enclosure, "Revolutionary Techniques." These were directions copied from the revolutionary literature of other countries. The "revolutionaries" were told how to provoke the police, how to avoid arrest, how to launch false rumours, how to behave in different situations, and so on. At that time, André Lavoie, 24, was supposed to be the editor. He was one of those who had not succeeded in getting into university (having been too arrogant at school), but he had taken a private course in journalism. However, a careful perusal of the journal shows that most of the articles must have been written by Pierre Vallières (who wrote far better than Lavoie). At the beginning of January 1966, Vallières proudly announced that there would be four different editions of *La Cognée:* a national edition, an edition for the workers *(édition syndicale),* an edition for university students and one for the high school students. The plan was, of course, much too ambitious. Only two numbers of each of the special editions actually came out. The aim of these papers was to turn the workers against the bosses, the students against the administration and the high school students against their teachers and parents. The subtitle of the high school edition read, "High school students, unite!"

All this, of course, was only a beginning. One cannot constantly inflame young people without providing proper targets for their aggression. In the high school edition (November 1965) a sentence said, "The crimes of our enemies call for violence."

However, all did not go well within the FLQ. In a letter signed "S.D." (Serge Demers?), the question was put to Paul Lemoyne (Vallières) as to why he alone was writing almost all the articles. The answer was very enlightening: There were only two writers left—"Paul Lemoyne" and "Louis Nadeau." The others had been assigned to another task (stealing dynamite?) (hold-ups?); two others had become the victims of cowardice or laziness; and the other three had taken to drink and no longer believed in the cause.

Meanwhile, the foot-folk grew restless and demanded to take part in spectacular actions. To these Vallières replied (15 March, 1966) in these terms:

> The FLQ, the bombs, the fireworks, that was the wonderful time! Things were happening in Quebec, it gave us the urge to get into the boat! We thought that something was going to happen at last. But today, the FLQ is nothing but a little paper *(une feuille de chou)* appearing every two weeks! These defeatist remarks one hears sometimes; others are on the point of saying it. No more bombs — no more FLQ, they think. But their impressions are quite unjustified. They are due to the silence the newspapers have wrapped around our actions for several months now.

But Vallières must have realized that his young friends could not be held back any longer. At the beginning of April 1966, the following order of the day was published in *La Cognée*:

> In order to attain our objectives: formation of a revolutionary party, creation of an indestructible striking force, the formation of manpower reserves, we demand, during the months ahead, a total commitment of all our militants and a faultless discipline.

Everybody knew then that great things were about to happen. After five months of revolutionary propaganda and preparation, the time for action had come. On Easter weekend (8 and 9 April, 1966), a strategy meeting took place at St. Philippe de Laprairie, in the home of Serge Demers whose mother happened to be away. It is highly improbable that Vallières and Charles Gagnon, the leaders of the group, should have been absent. Where else should they have been? In fact, Marcel Faulkner, one of those present, first said in court that both leaders were there. He later retracted his statement and it is obvious that the order had gone out to testify that Vallières and Gagnon were *not* at this high-level strategy conference. Apart from Vallières and Gagnon, there were five militants. At this meeting, the financial situation was discussed: more hold-ups were needed to provide the money for the full-time workers, break-ins were in order to get the necessary dynamite. And there is no doubt that the targets for the different attacks were chosen then and there. Already, some days before the meeting, members had broken into a quarry, unguarded at night, at South Stukely, Quebec and had got away with some dynamite.

On 15 April, *La Cognée* published new instructions on bombing techniques.

One week after the strategy meeting, 16 April, militants of the FLQ broke into a French-Canadian school, the Collège du Mont St. Louis in Montreal, where they stole a number of rifles, ammunition, some telescopes and other military equipment.

Two weeks later, the Cinéma Elysée in Montreal became the target of a robbery with arms. Mr. Serge Doyon, as good a French Canadian as any, was robbed of $2,400 on 1 May.

On 5 May, the terrorists killed their first victim: a French-Canadian lady of 64. The committee had decided to give a lesson to the owners of the strikebound Lagrenade shoe factory in Montreal. The "attack" had been decided at the Easter meeting, but had been postponed twice. Serge Demers had made the bomb. Accompanied by a juvenile, Gaetan Desrosiers, he brought the parcel which was addressed to the Vice-President. It was placed on the latter's desk. Some minutes later, Demers phoned the company that a bomb had been placed in their offices. But the management had already received so many threatening calls that they did not pay any attention. Moreover, the bomb was set to explode very soon and it is doubtful whether there would have been time to evacuate the premises. Miss Thérèse Morin had just come back from lunch when the bomb exploded in her face, killing her instantly. Three other persons were injured; the Vice-President got away with a broken arm. Two weeks after the bomb outrage, the shoe manufacturers of Quebec offered a reward of $2,500 to anyone giving pertinent information leading to the arrest of the terrorists.

It seems worthwhile to recall the situation at the H. B. Lagrenade Company. Like the textile industry, the shoe manufacturers of Quebec are up against extremely strong foreign competition. (More than 50% of our shoes are imported from Europe.) The Lagrenade factory was a small family business fighting against heavy odds. In the middle of April 1965, the CNTU had come to organize the workers who at that time earned $.90 (women) and $1.05 (men) per hour. The owners of the factory refused to deal with the union. They said there was no strike. Twenty workers stayed with the company and other workers were hired. Of the sixty-four workers who had left their jobs, forty-one had found work elsewhere. The remaining twenty-three continued on strike, meeting every work day in a dismal basement nearby, manning pickets, discussing the situation, and cashing strike money paid by the CNTU. It was a pretty hopeless situation because none of the parties wanted to give in. The owners maintained that with a union they might have a strike every year, which would force them out of business. The union would not accept defeat. There had been demonstrations by members of *Parti Pris* against the factory. The stalemate which the weekly *La Patrie* called "a strike dying of boredom" had thus lasted a full year when the FLQ intervened. The final effect of the bomb, apart from the killing, was to close the factory for good. Everybody was a loser. As for the leaders of the CNTU, they never took a stand for or against the FLQ action. (Since the Lagrenade bomb, most of the Quebec shoe factories have closed down.)

It took the FLQ about a month to inform its members of what they should think of the Lagrenade disaster. Finally, in *La Cognée* of 16 June, 1966, there appeared the following communiqué:

> *We are at the root of the attack against Lagrenade!*
> The political bureau of the FLQ considers that the moment has come to give a few explanations concerning the action of 5 May against the reactionary management of the Lagrenade company. Our silence since that day was justified by our desire not to embroil unnecessarily a situation already difficult for the population to understand. Following the approving silence of the leading unions, the positive neutrality of certain newspapers and the mercantile gesture of the managers of five shoe companies, the population of Quebec has understood that the right is on the side of the strikers, and that the family Lagrenade is first and foremost responsible for the accident which happened on that day. . . .
> The FLQ wishes to make it clear that the operation of 5 May was carried out under the direct suggestion of its leaders who want to assume the paternity and the responsibility of the action, despite the fact that their militants were not directly involved. We therefore advise the powers concerned—industrialists and policemen—that any action against its author will be considered as an action against the FLQ. We publicly assure the author of the action of our solidarity and our protection.

History repeats itself. We know that the author thus "publicly" protected was quite shaken by the outcome of the attack on Lagrenade. But, as in the first wave, he was faced with the argument: "We can't let ourselves be stopped because of one death. No revolution without bloodshed." The macabre merry-go-round had to continue.

In the meantime, on 18 May, 1966, a bomb exploded in a washroom of the Parliament Buildings in Ottawa. Paul Joseph Chartier of Toronto was killed by the premature explosion of a bomb he wanted to throw from the gallery into the Common's chamber. In the ninety-eight-year history of the Canadian Parliament this was the first instance of a violent act taking place in the Houses of Parliament. The bomb was meant as a protest and though it had nothing to do with the FLQ, it was certainly inspired by the violence in Montreal.

On 22 May, a bomb exploded near the factory of Dominion Textile at Drummondville, where a strike was in progress. There were only material losses.

The next bomb was more dangerous. On 3 June, it was deposited in one of the washrooms of the Centre Paul Sauvé, in Montreal, while a pre-election rally of the Liberal Party of the Province of Quebec was in progress. Prime Minister Lesage was there and most of the members of the Government. Fortunately, nobody was in the washroom when the bomb exploded.

The next incident was a vulgar hold-up in a private home, at 1578 Lavoie, Outremont. Serge Demers and Robert Lévesque, armed with rifles, stole $500 and a bottle of hard liquor on 9 June. (Robert Lévesque, 26, was an ex-convict of Kingston penitentiary who had lived on robberies for years.)

On 1 July (Dominion Day, Canada's national day), a bomb was made to explode near the City Hall of Westmount. The second victim of this wave was due now. It was a 16-year-old boy, Jean Corbo, son of a notary. While trying to place a bomb, according to Serge Demers' instructions, near the factory of Dominion Textile at 3970 St. Ambroise Street in Montreal, he was torn to pieces by a premature explosion. It happened on Bastille Day, 14 July, 1966. This particular factory was not on strike. Nobody else was hurt.

This time, Serge had had enough. He stopped manufacturing bombs. Without daring to quit the FLQ, he looked for a job and found work (ironically enough) on the Canada pavilion of Expo 67, then in construction. This made him technically a collaborator, but nobody seemed to mind. From then on, there were no more explosions. Some members, suspected by the police and wanted for questioning, left Montreal to hide at the FLQ camp at St. Alphonse, northwest of Joliette, fifty miles north of Montreal.

In fact, a summer camp had been rented near that community, to serve as a base for a new revolutionary army. Stolen dynamite, rifles, ammunition and other equipment were stored on the premises. The place was financed by hold-ups. (One of the terrorists told me he had participated in nine hold-ups of which only two were officially attributed to the FLQ.) The lease had been signed by a certain "François Marcelo." According to the handwriting expert of the Court of Sessions, this signature was in Pierre Vallières' handwriting. Vallières, at that time, was known as "Mathieu."

After an abortive hold-up at the French-Canadian-owned Cinema Jean-Talon in the east side of Montreal, on 27 August, 1966, a number of FLQ suspects were arrested. Twenty days later six young people were charged with murder.

Pierre Vallières and Charles Gagnon, wanted for questioning, had left Quebec for the USA. On 26 September, they both announced from New York that they had begun a hunger strike. Two days later they paraded before the UN building with big placards in French and English, protesting the arrest of their six comrades and trying to "attract the attention of the world to political repression in Quebec." Their publicity stunt was duly noted by the Quebec journals: the CBC even taped a TV interview. After which the two demonstrators were promptly arrested by New York police and imprisoned in Manhattan.

Their arrest caused a small group of intellectuals of the University of Montreal to come to their support. Philippe Decroix, Pierre Jauvin, Marie Lachance, Rev. John Proulx, Guy Sarrazin and Rev. Philippe Turcotte published a "Declaration of Solidarity" beginning with the following paragraph:

We declare ourselves solidly in support of the hunger strike undertaken by Pierre Vallières and Charles Gagnon in New York, 26 September, 1966. In this sense we fight for the liberation of the workers of Quebec. Moreover, we fight against any form of exploitation of man by man, and we try to promote a more just and more fraternal society through socialism. If Pierre Vallières and Charles Gagnon found it necessary to use violence in organizing the new terrorist FLQ network, they knew what they were doing. One may contest the realism and the efficiency of this method of action. One may just as well approve it. . . . Just as one can contest the realism of a world which the "decent people" believe to be peaceful when in fact it is based on the violence done each day to the weakest. . . !

This text seems characteristic of the confused sentimental thinking of intellectuals who have never worked with their hands in their lives but seem to know everything about the worker. Apart from the clear statement that Pierre Vallières and Charles Gagnon were the leaders of this FLQ group (and thus responsible for the hold-ups and the French-Canadian victims), the manifesto is full of generalities. On the question of violence it remains ambiguous.

In a second paragraph "neo-capitalism" is singled out as "the principal enemy of man." The third paragraph speaks of "establishing universal peace through fraternity" without saying how this noble goal is to be achieved. In a fourth paragraph, the authors state that "all lucid, responsible and fraternal men are fighting for the liberation of man." Whether the fight includes bombs or hold-ups is again left in suspense, and the authors do not find one word of sympathy for the poor innocent victims of this fight. It has always been easier to love humanity in the abstract than to love one's neighbour in everyday life.

Later, another paragraph was added in which the authors declared their opposition to the war in Vietnam. There at least, they were resolutely opposed to a mentality which tries to solve problems through violence.

The manifesto was published in *Quartier-Latin*, organ of the students of the (French) University of Montreal. It also appeared in *Le Devoir* of 28 October, 1966. The readers were invited to support the manifesto with their signature, in the offices of the *Quartier-Latin*. In all, 61 signatures were obtained, of which 41 came from members of the university. A breakdown of these signatures according to departments gives the following picture: Sociology and political science 13, philosophy and psychology 9, literature 5, law 3, other departments 4. Some signatures came from other universities. Four electricians and four mechanics had signed as representatives of militant workers, Madame Andrée Ferretti as representative of the RIN and Guy de Grasse as President of the "Committee for the aid to political prisoners." Considering that the number of students at the University of Montreal at that time was well over 10,000, the manifesto was hardly a success. Many people refrained from signing because of the ambiguity of the text which made it difficult to know whether their signature would or would not imply solidarity with the acts of violence of spring, 1966.

During his stay in Manhattan prison, Pierre Vallières wrote a book entitled *Nègres blancs d'Amérique* (*White Negroes of America*). We shall comment on this book later. On 13 January, 1967, Vallières and Gagnon were extradited from the USA and taken to Montreal to face charges of murder and manslaughter in connection with the 1966 incidents. Vallières was also accused of conspiracy in the bombing incident of 1 July, 1966 (Confederation Day), in Westmount.

The undercurrent of sympathy with the advocates of violence which had manifested itself in the aforementioned "Declaration of Solidarity" then became stronger. Stokely Carmichael sent a telegram in support of "the brothers of the FLQ." The executive of the nationalistic Union générale des étudiants du Québec (UGEQ) gave financial support to the cause of Vallières and Gagnon. (This Union is financed by the students of different universities, including McGill. It was doubtful whether the students would approve of such a use of their funds, but nobody protested. Later, the Union financed a march on McGill in favour of a "McGill français," and nobody protested then either!) The Aid Committee for the Vallières-Gagnon Group declared that Vallières and Gagnon were "innocent." The Committee failed to say who, then, did take "publicly" (and anonymously) the full responsibility for the fatal bombings. Nobody seemed to know now who the leaders were! In the meantime the courts tried to sort out the responsibilities.

Pierre Renaud, 23, on 23 September, 1966, pleaded guilty to a conspiracy charge concerning an FLQ hold-up. Perhaps owing to his charming manners, he received a suspended sentence. Two years later, we find him at the head of the Company of Young Canadians of the Province of Quebec, with several other ex-terrorists working under him.

On 13 June, 1967, exactly eleven months after the last bomb explosion, the following members of the Vallières-Gagnon group received these sentences:

Serge Demers, 22, thirteen offences: eight years and eight months.
Marcel Faulkner, 22, seven offences: six years and eight months.
Gérard Laquerre, 25, eight offences: six years and eight months.
André Lavoie, 23, four offences: three years and six months.
Claude Simard, 20, eight offences: five years and ten months.

The judge, Yves Cousineau, said that he had taken into account the serious nature of the crimes but also the fact that the offenders were young and gifted people whose future must not be destroyed. At a later date, Rhéal Mathieu was sentenced to nine years and two months, including one year for contempt of court. Finally, on 25 November, 1968, Robert Lévesque, 27, was sentenced to seven years for conspiracy in bombing attempts and hold-ups.

As to Pierre Vallières, he had already been sentenced, in April 1968, to life for non-qualified murder in the case of Thérèse Morin. He was not sentenced for having committed the act but for having inspired the outrage at Lagrenade by his writings, his actions and his attitude. The judge had good reason for saying this. The police had found detailed FLQ instructions for acts of violence dated March 1966. These instructions were written in the style of Pierre Vallières. Here are some extracts:

The arms cache of each group should include: one revolver for each member, cartridges, dynamite, detonators, acids, black powder, containers for the transportation of the bombs, clubs, saws, shovels, nails, screw drivers, wire etc. Moreover, each head of a group must have in his possession the instructions for the fabrication of Molotov cocktails. . . .

It may happen — and this will happen most certainly — that groups or members of a group will be called upon to use machineguns or grenades. In this case, these arms will always be furnished by those responsible for the detachment (four groups) who will see to it that the arms are returned as soon as the operation is terminated.

As one can see from these instructions, the FLQ of 1966 had even more dangerous things in store than planting bombs. To believe that Pierre Vallières knew nothing about this would be very naive. He and Charles Gagnon lived in the very house where the "attack" on Lagrenade was decided. Yet the game of innocence was being played with virtuosity, in the case of Vallières as well as in that of Gagnon, while the smaller fish had to plead guilty and go to jail.

As to Charles Gagnon, he was sentenced to two years for conspiracy in the hold-up attempt at the Jean-Talon theatre, in 1966. Both he and Vallières appealed their sentences. Gagnon was also indicted for having caused the deaths of Thérèse Morin and Jean Corbo. He pleaded Not guilty.

After Vallières' condemnation, there were a number of demonstrations. Three days after the verdict, 15 June, 1967, about sixty persons paraded before Bordeaux jail in Montreal, in protest against the sentence. In Paris, a group of French Canadians demonstrated before the "Maison du Québec," protesting against "political repression in Quebec." There are more than a thousand students and artists from Quebec studying in Paris, many with government grants.

The pressures of the Aid Committee for the Political Prisoners (as it called itself also) and the demonstrations in the street, before jails, and in court houses raised a question of principle. It is an accepted rule that the judiciary power, in order to function impartially, must be free from undue pressures, be it from the government or from the public in general, or from pressure groups. By having recourse to such pressures, and by appealing to emotions, the sympathizers seem to prove that they are not interested in justice *per se,* nor in a democracy functioning along the classic guidelines of *The*

Spirit of Law by Montesquieu. They can only conceive a justice at the service of one class — theirs.

According to the *Committee,* Gagnon was innocent. Yet this is what Charles Gagnon wrote on 3 May, 1968, from prison (the italics are ours):

> The people of Quebec are angry. Their apparent indolence is but suppressed anger. It needs only a spark to set it on fire. And it is precisely our role as a revolutionary spearhead to provide this spark. *We must put fire everywhere in Quebec. We must speak words of fire, do acts of fire, and escalate them.*

In the review *Socialisme* of November 1968, Charles Gagnon suggested illegal and criminal acts such as: occupations of schools or factories or buildings of the municipal and provincial authorities. He also proposed the creation of stocks of arms for the "resistance" ("We must think of this *now*") and of the immediate "organization of a perhaps clandestine revolutionary movement."

This open invitation to acts of violence was justified as follows:

> I think that we in Quebec are living just now in a particularly important period of our history. It is possible that if a real revolutionary movement does not come into being right now, we will remain for a long time in the rear guard of the contemporary Western revolutionary impulses, when we could be in the forefront of the revolution in North America. We must work for the revolution right now.

The inflammatory words of Charles Gagnon (We have not quoted everything!) raise some very important questions. Must we have a revolution because others have one? (One remembers that the French had a student revolt coupled with a general strike just when Gagnon wrote these lines.) What difference is there between a warmonger and an apologist of revolution? Is not a revolution, like any war, fought at the expense of women and children, of innocent victims? Is not a revolution, like any war, always considered "just" by those who start it, and is not the outcome generally quite different from what was promised? Indeed, nobody can say what a real revolution in Quebec would bring, nor where it would end. Like any war, it would be a gamble and bring misery to at least one generation. Obviously, neither Charles Gagnon, nor Vallières, nor the Aid Committee ever asked themselves those questions. But many Quebeckers do.

Gagnon's invitation to stockpile arms also deserves a comment. We remember that the second wave (ALQ) stole military equipment to the amount of over $50,000. In August 1964, the ill-starred hold-up at International Firearms caused the death of two people and sent five men to jail for life. On 15 June, 1965, *La Cognée* announced that "a commando" had stolen "a quantity of arms and ammunition" at St. Anastasie. On 4 December, 1967, a number of rifles and ammunition valued at $9,000 were taken from a sports shop at Cap de la Madeleine, a well-known place for pilgrimage. A note left behind said, "Thanks. FLQ." In the spring of 1969 about one hundred rifles and cases of ammunition were stolen in an arms' store in Montreal. The thieves had entered through the roof. Finally, taking advantage of the illegal strike of the Montreal police force, on 7 October, 1969, a gang broke into International Firearms, stealing twenty-five rifles. (After this second assault, the store went into liquidation. The FLQ had won, after all!) In the last three instances, the thieves have never been apprehended. In view of these facts, one can estimate that about three hundred rifles must be in the hands of the "revolutionary forces."

On 2 April, 1969, a jury of twelve persons found Charles Gagnon not guilty of the death of Jean Corbo. While the court was in session, demonstrations took place in front of the Court House. After the verdict, the Aid Committee for the Vallières-Gagnon Group issued the following communiqué:

Charles Gagnon is innocent!
The members of the jury after all were not fooled by the gambits, contortions and superhuman efforts of the Crown to get the head of a man. Nor were they fooled by proofs which were nothing of the sort, nor by perfidious insinuations. They have, in rendering

their verdict, stated that the fact of being a member of the FLQ does not constitute a crime. What exactly could one hold against Charles Gagnon? It can obviously be predicted that the Crown will appeal the decision of the twelve jurors. After all, this is its strict duty. . . . But the Crown should not believe that the people will let them spend money indefinitely in order to obtain the condemnation of an innocent man. This victory constitutes a transcendental step in the march of the Quebec people towards liberation.

Who *is* this man, aged 31, whom the newspapers call "a former lecturer of sociology at the University of Montreal"? It is certainly necessary to get an objective view of the life story of this controversial figure. For some, he is almost a hero, a leader in a mystic revolutionary march towards "liberation." Others are asking themselves whether he is not first and foremost a neurotic personality who, failing to give real meaning to his life and unable to make a satisfactory adjustment to society, became obsessed by the idea of revolution.

Charles Gagnon:
The Man and his Ideas

Charles Gagnon was born in February 1939 at Bic near Rimouski, Quebec, the youngest of fourteen children. His father was a farmer and woodcutter. Charles is the only revolutionary in the family.

He was the most intelligent of the whole family and had no difficulty making his way to the University of Montreal, after having finished his studies at the Seminary of Rimouski. But like many gifted young people, he had difficulty in finding his métier. He first studied French literature and linguistics, then turned to sociology. He might have had an academic career (He was actually teaching sociology as a lecturer for a short time), but he was mentally too restless to settle down. He never finished his studies. At one time he also taught at Valleyfield.

He belonged to almost every leftist party or society in Quebec, but none satisfied him. From 1963 on, he devoted most of his time to politics. He contributed articles to the review *Cité Libre* (whose editor at that time was Pierre Vallières), but the review soon folded up. Then, again with Vallières, he worked for the short-lived *Révolution québecoise* (founded in the fall of 1964), a socialist journal more radical than the *Cité Libre*. When the Union générale des étudiants du Québec was founded, he not only fully supported its policy of militant socialism and unilingualism, but also worked for it. He was again among the founders of an organization called Travailleurs étudiants du Québec (TEQ), a society devoted to familiarizing students with labour problems. (This organization is now known as Action sociale étudiante, and is subsidized by the Quebec government.) Finally, he was also active in the Mouvement de libération populaire (MPL) working for socialism and independence.

Like Vallières, Charles Gagnon is a gifted journalist who writes excellent French. Together with Vallières, he decided to come to the rescue of the FLQ when, after the failure of the Schirm group, the terrorist movement was in bad shape. Both Gagnon and Vallières felt that better planning, more discipline and more experience was needed. In 1965 they reorganized the FLQ network which was soon known as the Vallières-Gagnon group. Of the two, Vallières was the better organizer. Most directions betray his inimitable style, including a 100-page guidebook of revolutionary practices. Gagnon contributed articles to *La Cognée* (apparently under the pseudonym "Louis Nadeau"), but here, too, Vallières was the more prolific.

His brother Roland describes Charles Gagnon as a very introverted person. ("He never exteriorized himself.") His parents and his siblings never knew what went on within him. As we have seen, he could express himself best in writing, and when he was angry, but he had long periods of silence and perhaps of depression. There is also a narcissistic element, but less pronounced than in Vallières. Both, however, have one thing in common: They are not really satisfied with what they have achieved in life, and they blame society for it. Both have their periods of dejection and despondency and need very much the reassurance that hundreds of people are marching behind them. Their friends report that their morale is good, but frequent outbreaks of temper (in front of the court and elsewhere) seem to prove that their nerves are frayed. It is not easy to be a revolutionary at all times, and especially a revolutionary in Quebec. The adulation of young sympathizers is fine while it lasts, but it does not go deep. Then there is the thought of all the young people of the terrorist group who may be marked for life by a burden which they took enthusiastically upon themselves as long as they did not realize the full consequences. Both Gagnon and Vallières have never had the courage to take the responsibility for the training they gave to those young people. In order to save their own skin, they have taken the stand that these youngsters acted on their own.

Gagnon's parents did not know the role their son played in the "Vallières-Gagnon group," the FLQ of 1965-66. They were shocked to learn it through the papers and on TV. In 1966, Charles was 27 years old and engaged. His fiancée dropped him after the debacle and married someone else.

Like Vallières, but in a different way, Charles Gagnon is a dreamer. His vision is revolution in Quebec. For him there is no good will, no mutual comprehension between classes, between French and English, between young and old, and there is no evolution. It's the all-or-nothing principle in its most inhuman aspect. The theory, the political dogma, even the mere slogan are his reality. He lives intensely in this inner world of violent fantasy which he projects outside. Whoever walks behind him walks into a political dream world.

It was a dream to believe that anything would result from his demonstration in front of the UN building (representing the world) in September 1966. Both the alleged hunger strike and the demonstration looked so puerile that they could only impress his Québecois sympathizers.

From January 1966 to February 1970, Charles Gagnon was imprisoned in Bordeaux jail. First he was sentenced to two years for conspiracy in the affair of the abortive hold-up at the Jean-Talon movie theatre in Montreal. He appealed the sentence. Then he was accused of homicide in the case of Jean Corbo, killed by a bomb he was carrying. Gagnon was acquitted of that charge on 2 April, 1969. A third charge, of homicide in the case of Thérèse Morin, was rejected by a jury, on 10 December, 1969. Gagnon was released on bail on 20 February, 1970. The Montreal section of the CNTU had furnished the bail money of $2,500. Almost at once, Gagnon was invited to appear on two TV programmes of the French network of the CBC, and he gave several press conferences.

It is difficult for a layman to follow Charles Gagnon through the labyrinth of legal procedures during the years 1967-70. As far as I can see, his subversive ideas (even his invitation to crimes such as theft of arms, occupation of government buildings, the formation of a revolutionary army, and so on) were never the object of a criminal charge.

During his stay in Bordeaux prison, Charles Gagnon had several emotional upsets. He tried another hunger strike; he suddenly dismissed his lawyer (Mr. Robert Lemieux), only to take him back later. He wrote his friend Mr. Godbout a furious letter in which he attacked the President of the Committee for the Aid to the Vallières-Gagnon Group, Mr. Jacques Larue-Langlois in Montreal, calling him a clown, and calling his friends a "revolutionary rabble."

Charles Gagnon lives in extremes. He will be a revolutionary or a nobody. For, as we had seen above, everything for him is absolute, black or white. To keep such a man in a cell for years is, of course, a most senseless method of "correction." He can but cling to his revolutionary ideas, if only to keep his sanity and his self-respect, and to prevent a deep depression. Personally, I think that a confrontation with the relatives of Miss Morin, the parents of Jean Corbo and with Walter Leja would have done more for him than years of isolation and frustration.

Who Is Pierre Vallières?

For his friends and admirers, as well as for the authorities, Pierre Vallières is the most important and most influential leader the FLQ has ever had. For the first, he is a shining example of a typical French Canadian and son of a worker fighting the colonialist mentality of the English and, with it, the whole of the capitalist system. For the authorities, he is a man who believes in violence as the only means of overcoming the present society, the man who wrote that *spectacular actions* of a criminal order are necessary from time to time, if only for the sake of publicizing one's revolutionary aims.

There is in Pierre Vallières a strong element of narcissism (the same as in Cohn-Bendit or Stanley Gray, for example). At the age of 27, he wrote his autobiography. The following description of his life and development is almost entirely based on what he wrote himself, with additional information obtained from people who knew him in the past. Vallières' autobiography is not only a self-description, but also a self-justification, and it is this aspect that deserves critical assessment.

A further important source of information is the clandestine journal *La Cognée* where Vallières wrote most of the articles from 1965 till September 1966. There can be no doubt whatsoever that he approved not only of the bombs but also of the hold-ups necessary to finance the full-timers, and the base at St. Alphonse. It is true that he cautioned the young hotheads under him against too impulsive individual actions; on the other hand he issued detailed instructions about the centrally controlled use of violence. After his arrest, the word obviously went around that nobody should testify against him. This led to much obviously false testimony intended to make him appear innocent and even ignorant of what was going on in his own group.

When, in 1968, his autobiography *Nègres blancs d'Amérique* (*White Negroes of America*) was published by *Parti Pris* in Montreal, Pierre Vallières was 30 years old. The book was also printed and published by Maspéro in Paris, in 1969. Since then a German and an American translation have appeared as well.

White Negroes of America in more than one way resembles Hitler's autobiography *Mein Kampf*. Both books were written in prison, both are books of self-description and self-justification, both constitute a violent attack on the existing order and the legitimate authorities. And both are full of allusions to revolutionary literature and other eclectic readings which went to form the convictions of the author. Finally, both books are full of repetitions and therefore much too long, and both lead up to an apotheosis of an entirely new society based on one nation, one language, one ruling ideology — a mixture of nationalism and socialism at the same time. And, even more striking, the language is exactly the same — exalted, dynamic, full of a pathos which communicates that sense of urgency which makes the crowds demonstrate in the streets. It is a language which admits of no reflection, no objection, a language appealing to emotions, national complexes, individual and collective frustrations. It thereby alerts the instinct of self-preservation, the most powerful of all. Both books actually constitute one long tirade, one long contestation, one long indictment by a sort of self-appointed prosecutor — society being on the bench of the accused — followed by a glaring promise to make everything new, once the old society is in ruins. We know that Hitler's contestation *was* successful, but then he had three powerful accomplices: the complexes of a lost war, the depression years, and the pacifism of the Western powers. What has Pierre Vallières working for him?

Hitler promised to "liberate" Germany, if necessary by force, that is to give Germany back its identity (Germany being conceived as a colony exploited by the Allies and the Jews), and to create a reborn nationalistic Germany. Pierre Vallières appears as the champion of all French-Canadian frustrations and humiliations. He promises his disciples "to build a new order and new values which will create new men and will lead to a new humanism, for the first time in human history." It is noteworthy that it will be the new order which will automatically produce a new fraternal and selfless type of man, not the other way round.

For his admirers, his book is a bible. For us, it is a human document which must be respected despite some formal weaknesses. There is no doubt that the book is animated, on one hand, by the highest idealism, but on the other by the desire for revenge and by hatred. The book also allows us to follow the process of gradual alienation of a worker's son who had every opportunity of developing his gifts but who preferred to become a dropout. Going from revolt to revolt, from negation to negation, he finally became a professional revolutionary. Despite his superior intelligence and a remarkable mastery of the French language, he never made it to the university. We can see in his self-inflicted defeats a source of frustrations which he then projected upon, or identified with, the French-Canadian context. His revolutionary faith replaced the religion of his parents, a religion in which he only sees the degenerative and oppressive aspects. Whether posterity will consider him as a precursor or simply as an unhappy maladjusted individual entirely depends on the historical constellation. As the famous German psychiatrist Kretschmer once said, in quiet times we diagnose them, in times of upheaval they rule us.

The tragedy of Pierre Vallières, up to now, seems to lie in the fact that, wanting to live according to his own ideas, from the age of 12 on, and rejecting every compromise with society, he has virtually developed in a world of his own. Not accepting any advice from parents or teachers, he is self-taught, self-educated. Unfortunately, it is impossible to develop a harmonious personality based mainly on rejection and negation.

As to the validity of Vallières' political judgements and values, history will have the last word. All we can say is that the fruits were not encouraging: terrorist acts more puerile than intelligent; nine direct and indirect victims (five French Canadians, one with a French-Canadian mother, two men of foreign extraction, one pure-bred Anglo-Saxon); young people seduced by the mirage of a revolution, and possibly traumatized for the rest of their lives. Truly, it is not a very glorious balance.

Pierre Vallières was born on 22 February, 1938 in Montreal. He has two younger brothers, André and Raymond, who are very different from him. For a time the family lived on Gascon Street, not far from Hochelaga — a poor quarter. There were no playgrounds and the boys ganged together in the streets, committing all sorts of mischief. Both parents wanted to bring up their children decently. Fearing the bad influence of the neighbourhood, they decided to move to the other side of the river. The father bought a small house at Longueuil-Annexe, in a kind of bushland which later became the site of Ville Jacques Cartier. Although the house was small, the father improved it considerably in the course of years.

Pierre Vallières describes his father as a rather submissive man. He worked in the Angus yards of the Canadian Pacific Railway and was never out of work, not even during the depression years which brought so much misery to many families. But the resignation of his father, probably born out of life experience, revolted the son at the early age of 13. The example of his father, who was a most loyal worker, seemed to prove to the son that "the workers, in order to liberate themselves, must unite in order to overthrow this old order of things and of values."

One gets the impression that Pierre Vallières secretly admired his father for his qualities, while blaming him for not being revolutionary. In fact, the father did everything that his children should have better opportunities than he had had. He had been one of fourteen children and had been obliged to leave school at the end of grade four in order to work. Pierre's mother had had a better education, having finished grade nine. She would have gone further had it not been necessary for her to make a living. She was an office worker before she married. Her dream had been to become a teacher. Pierre seems to have hated his mother for being more than just the wife of a proletarian. He describes her as a person who was always thinking in terms of security and who was afraid of any violent changes, any rebellion. She accepted things as they were, while her son found almost everything unacceptable. This led to great tensions between the two, and she is reported to have said very often: "This boy makes me die a little more every day." (I hope that one day a woman will write a book on the mothers and wives of revolutionaries, the first victims of revolution.)

Unfortunately, Pierre's father died at the age of 53 of cancer, after having built an extra room so that Pierre might study undisturbed. This premature death was one more occasion for Pierre to revolt. He even blamed society for it — as if cancer made a distinction between the classes! The son who often made life unnecessarily difficult for both of his parents said later, "This deceased man taught me more, by his example and that of his people, than all the theoreticians of socialism."

It was for his sons that Mr. Vallières bought the little red and white house at 1197 St. Thomas Street, Longueuil-Annexe. It was a house in the style of that time, a wooden structure covered with tar paper which made the cabin look like a brick home. There were only three rooms: a common room that also contained the kitchen, a bedroom for the parents and little Raymond, and another bedroom for Pierre and André. At first, they had to pump the water behind the house but Father Vallières soon installed an electric pump. There was no misery; there was order and cleanliness, but the family had to live modestly. Every penny saved went into improving the home.

Pierre did not like school. Even in Montreal, he had played all sorts of tricks on the nuns who taught him. In Longueuil-Annexe he became even worse. He rejected his teachers. In his book he calls them "condescending," but one wonders whether a child would feel like that. After all, the teachers represented "law and order" as well as knowledge, and Pierre never liked law and order. He writes also, "As far as I remember, I never learned anything at school except to be ashamed of my condition." Here again, we can hardly accept this as being true. Most other children were no better off, many came from worse homes than Pierre. Moreover, since the boy never repeated a class, he must have been learning something! But we may believe him when he writes that he abhorred the words "obedience, love, virtue" and that he hated to have to say "Thank you."

At home, Pierre was no more obedient than at school. Here too, he refused to behave properly. He obviously wanted to remain a savage whom the missionaries would in vain try to civilize. He reports this remark, by his mother: "He has no gratitude, no respect whatever . . . what a life, to bring up children like him!" She decided to have him admitted to a secondary school at Longueuil, a school with a good name, directed by brothers.

Pierre was then 11 years old, an age when any normal child accepts the school chosen by the parents. Again the boy revolted. Although he did not know the school at all, he felt only too well that it was an institution with certain standards, a school where discipline was a must. He violently refused to attend classes there. He preferred a primary school nearby. The primary school was held in a real slum, the teacher was incompetent, and the pupils came mostly from low-class families. Pierre wanted to remain with these urchins who learned nothing, but were left to roam for hours in the wasteland around, without any supervision. His young comrades initiated him in their sexual games and when he was 12 a girl aged 15 shared her experiences with him.

These details are extremely important. They seem to prove that, having been a rebel during his childhood, Pierre took a decision of utmost importance at the age of 11 or 12. By refusing to go to a "decent school," he refused to be integrated into society. By his own decision he alienated himself, preferring the company of the neglected and alienated children of the neighbourhood to the society of children whose parents cared. Pierre later made it look as if he had then acted out of solidarity with the disinherited of this earth, though in fact he may have simply preferred the freedom and the society of boys and girls who did what they liked, plus a school which made no demands.

At 13 Pierre left primary school "as one leaves a prison." His parents did not ask him to go to work, as real proletarians would have done. A junior (classical) college had just been opened in the district and he was admitted there. He soon became first of his class. Yet in retrospect he will not admit anything good about that school. He seems to have hated every single teacher, as well as the whole curriculum. But he learned effortlessly and did his homework in a minimum of time, which left him with the necessary leisure to read enormously. During the summer he worked at a construction job. This allowed him, for the first time in his life, at the age of 14, to buy white shirts, new trousers, and a tie.

The summer following he was less lucky; he found no work. His mother suggested he learn English in order to become a bank clerk. His reaction was: "What do you want me to do in a bank? Be exploited in the best fashion? Be a slave in a white shirt?" His hatred of the college grew also. The teachers were "stupid," "fakes," if nothing worse. Having reached the age of 16, Pierre rejected his father as too docile (without being grateful for what he did for him), absolutely hated his mother (who wanted him to become somebody and be able to support himself), and his "pseudo-teachers," in short any authority, any guidance. He wanted to be his own master, his own teacher, his sole authority.

At that time he was acquainted with a girl, and even thought of marrying her. In order to take her to the cinema and give her presents, he stole money from his mother. He completely alienated himself from his parents and his brothers, to the point of refusing to speak to them. Since he did not listen to his teachers either, he had to educate himself. No wonder that at the age of 16½, he was, to use his own words, "completely mixed up."

It was summer again. This time, he found a job in a bank. He was 17 and seemed to like his work for when September came he decided to stay on instead of going back to school. Things went well till February 1955, when Pierre became "fed up" with banking. He returned to junior college where they took him back as if nothing had happened.

But ten months later, in December 1955, he revolted again. Unless his teachers came to the help of the workers "by burning their churches, their seminaries, their manses, their Cadillacs and the rest of it," he would reject them and refuse to co-operate. He became the leader of a group of dissatisfied students who, instead of studying, gathered in taverns, drinking and discussing without end. Under these conditions it is astonishing that he passed his exams in June 1956, but he did slip through. From then on, he would not accept any teaching except from himself.

A friend helped him to get a job in a French-Canadian brokerage firm. For two years, he worked there as a clerk, computing interests and dividends of widows, elderly couples, rich people, speculators. Two years; he never stayed so long in any other place. He describes the world of finance as an eerie, artificial and fantastic world. For him, this was strictly a world of exploitation. He found that his white-collar co-workers "were even more alienated than the factory workers and the farmers." ("Alienated" is one of Vallières' favourite terms. It means living apart from the mainstream of social, cultural, and national interests, and having nothing to say or to contribute.) He writes that during those two years, he did everything "to stir up a revolt in those clean and well-lit offices" against "this exploitation with clean hands and a respectable face." But his efforts were of no avail; all he could obtain were "vague sighs." He could not understand why people should not feel as he did. Seeing everything through the bias of his self-chosen alienation, he did not see that men and women with more life-experience than his own did not want to be drawn into a sterile revolt by a young man who had never finished his studies and wanted to teach them how to live.

Pierre, for his part, exploited his boss from time to time by saying he was sick, when in fact he had gone to a tavern to discuss revolution with his friends. He also wrote a novel which was never published. Apparently it was a rather narcissistic self-portrait and an attempt at self-analysis.

After two years of office work, having some money put aside, Pierre decided to move on. He was "fed up" once more, fed up with "Montreal and the grey atmosphere of Quebec." He travelled to New York which was quite a revelation to him. He broke all ties with his family. In search of a new father-figure, he discovered Gaston Miron, a French-Canadian poet whom he calls "the spiritual father of the FLQ, of *Parti Pris*, of Quebec Revolution." Under the influence of this remarkable writer, Pierre began to write his first newspaper articles, published in *Le Devoir* in 1957, articles in which he calls the old generation "*les vieux croulants*," (the old decrepit ones).

Apart from Miron, Pierre found some other father-figures. He admired Jacques Ferron, the local doctor who treated the poor free of charge and later became a well-known writer. He looked up to René Lévesque, Gérard Pelletier, Jean-Louis Gagnon, Pierre Elliot Trudeau, André Langevin, Jacques Hébert. He also admired one woman — Judith Jasmin. These were the models he needed to guard him against his inner chaos, for, as he says himself, "I lived with my instincts and the monsters within." He read a lot: philosophy, poetry, literature, politics, anything that might provide him with a principle around which to organize his inner turmoil.

His first novel, entitled *Dark Nuptials* was refused by the French publisher because of its "ferociously immoral" end. He burned the manuscript (1958). He began another book, *The Demons*, and destroyed it as soon as it was finished. Despite the double holocaust, confusion continued to reign. For a short while, he had a passionate affair with a married woman. This was followed by the writing of a third novel, *The Drawers of Water*. He says that writing has the effect of a drug on him, and that, in this novel, he tried to "transform into vivid colours, red, yellow and green, the great blackness of life in Quebec."

It seems that Pierre Vallières, in this, was a precursor of the disciples of LSD. He was also a precursor of Hubert Aquin, whose best seller, *Trou de Mémoire*, achieved what Vallières only intended to do. Just before Easter 1958 the third novel also was incinerated, after which the author bought a bunch of flowers for his mother. But she seemed little impressed by a gesture which was as sincere as it was surprising.

Pierre asked himself why he was born. He felt "confusedly guilty — or responsible." Since he was unable to invest his uncommitted idealism in Quebec, he was, with all his heart, behind "the Algerian and Cuban partisans."

He was then 18 years of age. Three manuscripts lay in ashes behind him, liberating him — leaving him ready for something entirely new. Submerged by what Freud called "an oceanic feeling," he rushed into a "religious life" and became a novice of the Franciscan order. He read Kierkegaard, the great but neurotic philosopher who founded existentialism. He tried "to get hold of God" in a mystical way and "to make him speak up." This religious episode lasted over a year, but then Pierre again revolted (or became "fed up"). With a curse ("Masturbez-vous, Seigneur") he threw away his "religious life" like a dirty rag.

Later, the psychologist Andrée Benoist (whom we have mentioned earlier in connection with Edmond Guénette) explained to Pierre why he had wanted to become a Franciscan monk. According to her, he had actually desired to be reconciled with his family, his environment and its traditional values "because [his] revolt had not yet reached a sufficient degree of consciousness to be above the guilt feelings created by the 'morbid universe of Sin' characteristic of the Quebec ruled by the clergy."

It would be difficult to overvalue the importance of this step. Faced with a decision between the traditional values of his parents and the alienation of the rebel, Pierre chose the latter, assisted this time by a woman psychologist. As if one could get rid so easily of the values one was brought up in, as if one could live as a human being without feeling responsibility toward society! As if our superego, our conscience as a responsible human being were only based on outdated, imbecile notions either of our parents or of the church! It may well be the fundamental mistake of Pierre Vallières, and of the whole FLQ, to put oneself and one's personal ideas into the centre of the universe in an arrogant attempt to replace the divine order by the chaotic self-will of an inflated ego.

Pierre was no happier for his decision. In 1961, he accepted a job at the bookstore of the University of Montreal. One would have expected that selling books to young people (many of whom were separatists) would satisfy him. But after a few months, he revolted again and quit. ("I was fed up with selling books.") Soon afterwards, in September 1962, he even became fed up with Quebec and left for France with the intention of never coming back. In France, he first worked in the country for three months, then went up to Paris. He found no work there and lived first with some French Canadians, then with a couple from Martinique. The man was a defrocked priest who worked as an automobile mechanic. His common-law wife was described as a very sensitive young woman who finally advised Pierre to return to Quebec. Indeed, Pierre had not found any new insights in France. He had become very depressed, had suicidal thoughts. Having become a burden to his friends, the 25-year-old Pierre Vallières had to ask his mother to send him the money for his return to Canada. He arrived in Montreal in March 1963, a few days before the destruction of the Wolfe monument in Quebec which marked the beginning of the first FLQ wave.

A friend got him a job at *La Presse*, the great French-Canadian daily, as a journalist. But Pierre Vallières sometimes neglected his work in favour of demonstrations of all sorts.

Vallières also wrote a few articles for a dynamic political monthly called *Cité Libre*, founded in 1950 by Pierre Elliot Trudeau to fight political stagnation in Quebec in general and the paternalistic regime of Duplessis in particular. After the latter died in 1962, the review was looking for new objectives (which were not lacking) and also for new directors. In the summer of 1963, Trudeau and co-director Gérard Pelletier decided to turn it over to Pierre Vallières and Charles Gagnon. The change became effective in December 1963, but six months later both were dismissed.

Vallières then joined the Mouvement de libération populaire (MLP). He also founded, together with Gagnon, a new review, *Révolution québecoise*, which was not successful. In the fall of 1965, the MLP disbanded (though it was revived later) and the new FLQ (sometimes called the neo-FLQ) was founded instead, directed by Vallières and Gagnon. The main concern of the two leaders was to build a revolutionary organization and to edit the clandestine paper *La Cognée*. This paper had had a fitful existence ever since the first FLQ, but it had languished. With the takeover by Vallières and Gagnon, it immediately took on a vigorous new look. The only drawback of this mimeographed "organ of the FLQ" was its clandestinity ("It must not fall into the hands of police") which robbed it of most of its influence.

After the arrest of the members of the FLQ 1965-66, Vallières and Gagnon launched their hunger strike and wound up in Bordeaux jail in Montreal (January 1967). Here Vallières wrote, "The prison does not mean that I put on ice my political and social commitment. . . . A revolutionary must be ready to start again." A revolutionary has to learn to live dangerously. He rejects any idea of a compromise with the powers that be. Vallières felt that if he compromised it "would mean I had killed our ideal in my spirit and in my heart. Then, my friends might just as well bury me."

During his activities at the head of the FLQ of 1965-66, Pierre Vallières wrote a great deal. This is confirmed by Mrs. Demers, in whose house he lived for about two months. She considered him a writer without knowing what it was he was writing, nor that her son was involved in his activities.

Vallières was 26 years old when he was the leader of the Vallières-Gagnon group. From his writings of that time we can say that he tried to give his young disciples a kind of revolutionary training. He used a kind of revolutionary guidebook entitled *What is the FLQ?*, describing revolutionary tactics, from demonstration and defiance of police to the manufacturing of bombs, the use of arms, and so forth.

While enflaming the young with his prose, he also was obliged to warn them not to engage in rash actions which could lead to a catastrophe. There is no doubt that he had great authority and that his words were heeded. This is so true that it is most unlikely that the bombing at Lagrenade should have been carried out without his approval. He must also have agreed with the many hold-ups necessary to finance the movement (and himself?). Yet he later brazenly maintained his innocence. Such was the effect of his propaganda that the great majority of the French-Canadian public actually came to believe that he was persecuted solely for his political beliefs, not for any leading role in the actions of the neo-FLQ.

As far as his political ideas were concerned, they are on two different levels: theory and practice. In *La Cognée* and in his general instructions the theory is only implicit. It is taken as self-evident that only a revolution can bring about a reign of social justice and fraternal equality. No change without violence! The present regime must be attacked and vanquished by force, Castro fashion. The FLQ was to be the trigger, the detonator, which would set fire to the exploited masses of Quebec. Clandestinity, illegality, criminal methods of action were justified by the end. This was the practical faith which Pierre Vallières propagated indefatigably, mainly through *La Cognée*. After the arrest of his group, he expressed the same ideas in his *White Negroes of America* (1968), where he mentions dynamite and guns as weapons of combat:

> We have to form groups and to settle accounts, once and for all, with the whole gang of those damned heartless exploiters. . . . There is enough dynamite in Quebec to blow up all of them.
> It will be the turn of the millionnaires and militarists to taste blood — their own blood.
> After all, guns can be used for something else but hunting. . . .

Pierre Vallières identifies himself completely with the FLQ. He writes, "We of the FLQ" had to opt "at the end of 1965, for clandestinity."

For all its clandestinity, Pierre Vallières explains, the FLQ did not frown upon legal actions, such as demonstrations. These actions were undertaken in order to radicalize the demands of workers and students, and to make the FLQ popular in their ranks.

FLQ militants were young, from 16 to 30 years of age. Some of the members had already worked in labour unions or in radical movements, others were new to politics and only motivated by the desire "to get things going." The FLQ, though a terrorist movement, was not motivated by "blind passions," by the love of adventure *per se*, by nihilism or the longing for martyrdom; on the contrary, they said, "We know with a certain precision what we want."

Towards the end of 1965, the FLQ opted once more in favour of clandestinity. As in the first FLQ of 1963, the cells would operate fairly independently (although according to some master plan), the members of one cell should know those of another cell only by code names. Names, addresses, meetings, as well as those attending them should be kept absolutely secret. Parents should never be told anything. Members would have to live a double life. On the surface, they would be common citizens going about their work like everyone else, while secretly preparing the illegal actions of the FLQ. The beginners should first distribute tracts, print clandestine papers and pass them on to friendly college students and others. They would also have to study certain books and learn how to initiate discussions or make little speeches in a circle of friends. By doing this and by demonstrating in the street, they would learn to overcome their initial shyness. Then they would progress to picketing during strikes, to affronting the police with clenched fists, to defying their bosses, and so on. The last step, of course, would be the thefts of dynamite, the bank hold-ups, and the manufacturing of bombs — activities reserved for those who had proven their worth in the preliminary fields mentioned above.

Pierre Vallières considers himself a professional revolutionary, ready to die "for that human ideal which has become the very reason of our existence." He will say, "I cannot live my life without working at making a revolution." In his *White Negroes,* he explains in detail the origins of his revolutionary philosophy. In fact, he is the only leader of the FLQ who ever seriously attempted to give a philosophic foundation to his revolutionary aspirations. This is perhaps due to his Catholic education: he was looking for a faith which would also appeal to reason. Pierre Vallières takes the Marxist materialism for granted: the spirit, the philosophy, the aspirations and the morality of man are but the reflection of the particular economic system in which he lives. Under a rotten economic system, man is rotten. To turn the economic and political system upside down leads automatically to a complete change of the character, the mentality, the outlook, the philosophy of man. Pierre Vallières is not in the least embarrassed by the fact that the Russian experiment has failed to produce the new man. He explains the failure simply by saying that the Russians have merely replaced monopolistic capitalism by state-capitalism, which means they have not gone far enough.

Because Pierre Vallières believes in the unproven dogma of the supremacy of matter over the spirit, he conceives man not as *homo faber,* but as *homo oeconomicus.* The supremacy of matter also implies the supremacy of violence over peaceful discussion, the supremacy of revolution over evolution, the supremacy of the materially strong and the terrorist methods over other methods of persuasion. It is a world in which violence, guns and bombs are the most powerful agents of change.

Marx never believed in the value of the individual, nor in the reality of free will. He always thought in terms of masses. Even the leaders only express what the masses think and feel and want. The *Internationale* appeals to the masses and to mass instincts. Pierre Vallières does likewise.

Pierre Vallières' fundamental materialism is clearly expressed in passages like the following: "The most elementary rights of man demand a global revolution, not in the minds or in the mentality of people, but of the social relationships, the mode of production on which is based and out of which grows any 'mentality'."

Yet the materialism of Pierre Vallières sounds strangely familiar to anyone living on the American continent. After all, what difference is there between Marxist materialism and the materialism of North America? Do not the North Americans believe in the supremacy of matter over spirit, of money over ideas, of techniques over humanity? The American continent is impregnated with the materialistic philosophy which puts technical achievements before spiritual excellence. The most American of all philosophies, pragmatism, is essentially the surrender of the human spirit before a materialistic environment. And if the French-speaking people of Quebec have one great advantage over the 200 million English-speaking, it is that of being totally different. Indeed, the tiny fraction of 5 million French-speaking in a sea of 200 million English-speaking can only survive if they distinguish themselves by the force and newness of their ideas, by their particular spirit, by the originality of their artistic creativity and the brilliance of a language which is so beautiful and expressive that all the others will want to learn it.

If the Québecois just try to be as materialistic as the rest of North America, if they are just satisfied with making and driving the same cars on the same super highways, in having the same salaries, wearing the same clothes, using the same business tricks, sharing the same outdated trade-union concepts, the same infantile idea of liberty as licence they might just as well share the language. It is not by *speaking* but by *thinking* differently, by evolving a distinct image of man, by developing a squarely un-American life-philosophy based on spiritual values that Quebec can become unique and even of vital importance to a continent which is sick. This would automatically give Quebec its particular status and an influence far greater than one would expect from its size of population. Thus, even the idea of political independence (also based on materialistic concepts) might become irrelevant.

Class war, violent revolution, socialism are not the solution to Quebec's problems. What advantage is there in replacing the hegemony of one class by the dictatorship of another, or capitalist materialism by dialectical materialism? The experiment has been tried in a number of countries, but the results are anything but convincing. It is because of this failure that Pierre Vallières proposes to go further and to do better than the existing "socialist countries."

As we have said already, Pierre Vallières has an eclectic mind. His favourite Marxist authors are the young Marx (with his "tonifying thoughts"), Georges Lukacs ("orthodox Marxism") and Karl Korsch. All three authors are actually rejected by the communist regimes of Europe. The writings of young Marx are excluded from his "complete" works as printed in Russia; both Lukacs and Korsch have been labelled heretics by the 3rd International. Lukacs was a Hungarian Jew who played a part in the Bela Kun communist regime in Hungary, from 1920 to 1921. After the demise of this regime (which did not last because it was not backed by a powerful Russian army), he went to Vienna where he wrote his most important work, *History and Class Consciousness* (1923). This book, characterized by a great idealism, was declared a heresy by the 3rd International because it contradicted some of the theories expressed in Lenin's *Materialism and Empirio-criticism,* the bible of Russian communism. The work of Lukacs culminates in a sort of apocalyptical vision: a global revolution sweeping the world, obviously an aspect which would attract Pierre Vallières. However, Lukacs was obliged to publicly retract some of his ideas. In 1956, he took part in the Hungarian revolution against Russia and after the defeat of that revolution he was deported to Rumania, though he was allowed to go back to Hungary some years ago. In 1970 he was 85 years of age.

Karl Korsch is a German communist of the very first days, and a very independent spirit. His principal book, *Marxism and Philosophy* in many ways resembles Lukacs' work. It shared the same fate of being outlawed by the 3rd International. Soon afterwards, in 1925, Korsch had the courage to denounce "red imperialism." He was promptly ejected from the German communist party. At that time, there was a movement among Russian workers which aimed to give the workers a voice in the decisions of the Party. Korsch was in contact with this movement which was crushed by Stalin. In 1933, Korsch left Germany and in 1936 was able to emigrate to the USA. Despite the fact that he refrained from all political activities, Soviet agents tracked him down in America and tried to mete out to him the same fate which befell Trotsky. The "heretical" ideas of Lukacs and of Korsch were inspired by humanitarian and democratic ideals not very different from those which Dubček tried to realize in Czechoslovakia in 1968. Indeed, both Lukacs and Korsch had great confidence in the worker and his good judgement, while the Soviets did not believe in any form of co-operation, but used the workers as instruments to be manipulated through the censorship of the press and the official propaganda. It must be said that the German or Hungarian worker, having been brought up in a freer society, had a better and more independent political judgement than the Russian worker.

Vallières takes the side of Lukacs and Korsch and blames the Russians for not having "integrated" the worker in the revolutionary process. Instead of participating in the political and economical development of the country, the Russian workers are "obliged to obey precise orders formulated by a central committee which considers itself infallible." Soviet society does not allow anyone to question the power of the ruling class or the established order. For Pierre Vallières, this is wrong. Revolution should be permanent: "The new society, too, is an incomplete society." It should remain flexible, open to change. Marxism and the official Soviet teachings are two different things. For Vallières, Marxism is "not a finished system, not even one that could be finished." It is a method of thinking and acting which should not be petrified. It is by acting that one gives a meaning to one's life, "action conceived as a commitment" and leading to "total liberation." In other words, as Marx said, the aim is "to transform the world." This transformation never stops. "To transform the world is to understand and explain it — a unique process, indivisible, lived by us all."

Pierre Vallières, no doubt, has very high ideals. At the same time, he is motivated by hate and resentment. He wants to revenge his father, as it were. This mixture of idealism and resentment can be found in many revolutionaries; it was characteristic of most members of the FLQ. No wonder Vallières' philosophy appealed (and still appeals) to many young people. A young man who does not want to transform the world has become prematurely old. But then there is the question of how to go about it. The weakness of the FLQ is to use inferior means to achieve lofty goals. Personal complexes, as we have seen already, may provide a lot of energy, but this energy will be destructive rather than creative. Resentment prevents objective judgement. Hate makes blind. Where there is subjectivism, there is danger of oversimplification.

For Vallières, the young are good, the old either stupid or bad. He believes in class war, in the "good" worker and the "bad" boss. He sees nothing but exploited and exploiters everywhere (even the students are exploited!). Like Plato two thousand years before him, he believes that money should be abolished, since money makes people greedy and selfish. Everyone should receive according to his needs. All this sounds wonderful, but the abolition of money would still not eliminate the struggle for power of which the struggle for money is only one aspect. To abolish free commerce and the values determined by supply and demand would make the individual totally dependent on the state, the only giver of things. It could well be that the last condition of the citizen would be worse than the first.

In 1833, a young Polish poet gave the classical answer to those who think they can remake the world by violence. In a play called *Undivine Comedy,* the 21-year-old Polish poet Krasinski described such a revolution. His famous dialogue between Citizen-leader Pancrace and Count Henry could have been written today. Pancrace

(The name means "Master of all") proclaims, "I recognize but one law, before which I bow. It is a law which hurls the world into ever higher spheres. This law proclaims your doom. Through my mouth, it speaks right now: 'You — the rotten ones, the decrepit full of drink and food, give way to the young, to the hungry, to the strong'." To which Henry replies, "I know you and your new world. I have seen, in the shades of the night, the crowd dancing and shouting. On their shoulders you have climbed to power. I have seen all the old crimes of the world, clad in new garments, sing a new song. It all will end up as it always did: in lust, cupidity, and blood."

One cannot doubt the sincerity of Pierre Vallières. His ideas must be taken very seriously. That is why we have given them so much space here. Many young people think as he does, many believe that it is sufficient to destroy a system to have the guarantee of a better one. Yet Joseph Conrad once criticized "the imbecile and atrocious answer of a purely Utopian revolution encompassing destruction by the first means to hand, in the strange conviction that a fundamental change of heart must follow the downfall of any given human institution. These people are unable to see that all they can effect is merely a change of names."

Vallières also calls biology to his aid. He writes that life itself is based on contradictions which lead to revolutions, that even in a living cell there are chemical reactions (of a revolutionary order?). This would be fine if a closer look did not reveal that the testimony of nature contradicts the allegations of our revolutionary. The chemical changes within the living cell have no other aim but to preserve the status quo. The cell is a perfect example of a harmonious and interdependent society. There is even a police: the white blood cells are mobilized as soon as there is trouble; they all converge to "re-establish order." The same thing holds true of nature. Every upheaval, every "revolution" here is rather a catastrophe than a natural process. Inundations, earthquakes, land slides, forest fires, and so on are destructive. Decidedly, nature is not on the side of Pierre Vallières, for nature believes in evolution. There is but one real "revolution" in the course of life: the birth of a new individual. But even here, nature proceeds quite differently from our revolutionaries: the new condition is prepared carefully, in every detail. The lungs are ready to function at a moment's notice, the digestive system is prepared to receive its first food. And the violence which pushes the baby into the world is sufficiently moderated to protect the child as well as the mother. Finally, the latter is not disposed of in favour of the "new generation." On the contrary, a most harmonious symbiosis is established between the two generations.

If biology does not provide any proofs supporting the theory of the "necessary revolution" (or even of the necessity of class war, generation war, and so forth), the historical proofs are not less doubtful. Marx himself could only name five examples of class war upheavals over a period of two thousand years. Moreover, most of these "revolutions" somehow went wrong. It is a fact that nearly all successful violent revolutions (with the single exception of the American War of Independence) have not led to a "liberation," but to a dictatorship of some kind. The quiet revolutions, the spiritual upheavals such as the Renaissance, the Reformation, the insight of enlightened individuals, and technical progress have done far more for the liberation of mankind than any violent revolution.

It is indeed difficult to understand how intolerance, hate and destruction could lead to tolerance, fraternal love and the construction of a better society. The same people who are against the war in Vietnam are in favour of civil war in Quebec. The same people who violently demonstrate against the racism between black and white will foster a virulent racism between French and English. One is against the legitimate "fathers," but idolizes paternal figures such as Mao or Ho-Chi Minh. One is against the existing democratic system, but at the same time demands the democratic right to demonstrate at any time or to disseminate inflammatory literature. One is against the law (because the law is Ottawa), but uses every crack and cranny of this law to one's own advantage.

Pierre Vallières was sentenced to life on 5 April, 1968, but in 1969 the sentence was quashed. On 18 December, 1969, he was again convicted of involuntary homicide, and condemned to thirty months by Judge Miquelon. He appealed again and got out on bail in May.

Vallières was not the idol of every FLQ partisan. For this we have the testimony of *La Cognée* of October 1966 (No. 62). At that time, Vallières and Gagnon were imprisoned in New York, and *La Cognée* was edited by someone else. This is what the new editor wrote:

> We are not associated with the Vallières-Gagnon group . . . both had found that *La Cognée* as well as the FLQ were good business in a symbolic way, and they had taken over. However, we do not disapprove of the operation Lagrenade which they carried through well and which in every respect was a complete success [sic], the death of an old spinster being due to the criminal obstinacy of her bosses not to take note of a certain telephone warning.

The same editor also wrote a letter of apology to the parents of young Jean Corbo — the only instance known where the FLQ ever apologized for its acts. At the same time, the new editor blamed Vallières for having encouraged 16-year-old boys to take part in such dangerous actions.

The Other Partisans of the Neo-FLQ

Apart from Vallières and Gagnon who were undoubtedly its leaders and in more than one way its mentors, the FLQ group of 1965-66 had a hard core of seven members. Two of these were 19, two others 21, the fifth 23 and the two others 24. All except one had had a most normal upbringing.

The only exception to the general pattern was a young man of 21, of comparatively low intelligence. He had lost his father when he was very young, and had great difficulties at school (he is still a very poor speller). He became a consistent truant and was finally sent to Reform School. After he left there, he never kept a job for very long, and hung around in the company of beatniks and misfits. He was apparently attracted to the FLQ by a spirit of adventure and a desire to boost his ego. He was particularly good at hold-ups, where he could overcome his feelings of inferiority and where he felt accepted, if not admired. Without doubt, this young man had personal weaknesses which the group exploited without scruple. As far as he was concerned, he believed he had found the cure for his previous failures in the excitement of the clandestine FLQ activities.

Another member who did not conform to the norm was Robert Lévesque, who had a long criminal record of robberies. Liberated from Kingston penitentiary in 1964, he had gone to Montreal and become involved with the FLQ. Because of his former experience, he must have taken part in a number of FLQ hold-ups, including one in a private home.

The other five members of the group had experienced less difficulty at school. One, it is true, was expelled from a junior college because of arrogant behaviour, and had to be content with a private course in journalism. (He later contributed to *La Cognée*.) Two others went to university. One of them was preparing his B.SC. The fourth and the fifth could also have gone to university, but were working temporarily. During the winter 1965-66, all the members of the group were either working full- or part-time for the FLQ. They read a lot, discussed the political issues, took part in demonstrations, followed closely public events, especially in the field of labour conflicts. Every strike for them was a sign of the coming revolution.

Apart from the hard core, there were other partisans who were considered as apprentices: two juveniles aged 16 and a number of sympathizers who gravitated around the group and were avid readers of *La Cognée*. The group itself was divided into several subgroups. A group of three specialized mainly in thefts of dynamite, another group in hold-ups, others were mainly busy with the journal. Serge Demers was the bomb-maker. Vallières and Gagnon supervised the whole proceedings and wrote for the paper.

There are two aspects of this situation which strike the historian: the complete lack of scruple underlying these activities, and the juvenile mentality of the participants. Perhaps the most juvenile of all the terrorist acts perpetrated by this group was the idea of blowing up the statue of the French-Canadian patriot Dollard des Ormeaux, standing in Lafontaine Park. Before the outrage, which happened on the Queen's Birthday, a poster with the inscription "Long live English Canada" was placed nearby. The terrorists hoped that the destruction of the monument would be imputed to the English and that French Canada would be swept by a wave of hatred against the English out to destroy their hero. In fact, Dollard des Ormeaux refused to budge despite the explosion and nobody took the idea of a sinister English plot seriously.

As to the absence of scruple, it has always been typical of all FLQ groups. It is a psychological fact that within a group of conspirators, individual responsibility only exists towards the group and never with respect to society at large. It is the group which commands, which takes the responsibility. It is to the group one must be loyal and it is the group which is the beneficiary of all illegal acts, especially of the hold-ups. The clandestinity contributes a great deal to this group morality. Since everything is done by the group and for the group (and, through the group, for the "people"), the individual by necessity finds it unjust to be sentenced as a fully responsible person. By the same token, each member will deny having acted criminally, since he acted loyally towards his friends. All the morality is concentrated within the group; for the outside world (including the parents, brothers and sisters) lies, falsehoods, thefts and treason are considered as a perfectly legitimate means of behaviour. Thus the group offers the immature individual the illusion to act like a "man." In a group which in advance absolves its members from all blame, even the timid may become reckless.

Serge the Bomb-maker

Whether you like it or not, when you commit certain acts which make headlines, you become a public figure. Serge had publicly to render account before the judge, in the presence of dozens of journalists. His full name had been in print over a hundred times. Knowing Serge as a sensitive and rather introverted young man, I can assess the anguish caused by this periodic publicity. He never denied being the bomb-maker of the group. He admitted that it was he who, accompanied by his friend Gaetan Desrosiers, had brought the bomb to the Lagrenade shoe factory. He also admitted that he had given another bomb to 16-year-old Jean Corbo, instructing him how to set the timing before placing it. Both bombs had caused the death of a person.

On the other hand, Serge had always disliked the hold-ups which placed the FLQ on the same level with professional criminals. Yet he took part in one.

Perhaps because the famous summit meeting of Easter 1966 took place in Serge's home, the police considered him wrongly as a key man. They tried by every means to gain his confidence and to cajole him into telling them the secrets of the Vallières-Gagnon group. They offered him good meals, took him home to see his mother — all in vain. About certain things, Serge would not speak. He would admit what *he* had done, but would not betray others. Let them speak for themselves!

Since Serge had introduced Vallières and Gagnon to his unsuspecting mother, who had rented them a room with board, he must have known a good deal about the role of these two men, and the police knew that he knew. Finally, considering his refusal to speak, the judge declared him a hostile witness. Moreover, Serge was charged with perjury. For over two years, he has been called to court every two or three months, where he has pleaded "Not guilty," after which the case has been postponed. And each time, the press has reported the event. The case was finally dismissed in 1970, and Serge became eligible for parole.

If Serge had been born in 1935 instead of 1945, he would not have become the victim of revolutionism. He was an asthmatic and frail child, unable to practise sports. Instead, he loved to read. He is intelligent, had no difficulty at school, finished grade eleven in Syracuse, N.Y., where he became fluent in English. He is not animated by that irrational anti-American hate which characterizes so many FLQ, and he is not a doctrinaire. He is such a likable, well-adjusted and well-mannered young man (no vulgar *joual* spoken here!) that one is reluctant to call him a revolutionist or a terrorist. That he was responsible for two deaths is one of those contradictions mentioned by Pierre Vallières himself, contradiction which another FLQ man characterized by saying: "I must be violent because I love."

It took me a long time to discover the real motives which moved this sympathetic and sensitive young man to become a bomb-maker. The story I am going to tell I do not have from him (although I know him personally), but from other sources.

Serge was born in 1945. He has a younger brother. His father was a maintenance worker in a factory. Being a militant unionist, he became president of the local union, comprising a few hundred workers. In 1963, the company dismissed him, after fifteen years of faithful service. Being well over forty, he found it impossible to join another company, but he was able to make a living by working on his own account, installing aluminum sidings.

Through his father, Serge very early became interested in labour questions. The fact that his father had lost his job, obviously because he was the president of the shop union, and the role of union rivalry (American unions as against Quebec unions) made him very bitter.

Indeed, the company decided to contract out the maintenance work, to dismiss its own maintenance workers and let members of another union do the job. It would certainly have been easy for the company to find another job for Serge's father, but no effort was made to do so. The new maintenance workers belonged to a small independent union, member of the Association of Independent Unions in Montreal, directed by Mr. Lucien Tremblay. (The Neo-FLQ believed that the very same association had provided workers for the Seven-Up plant in 1965 and for Lagrenade shoe factory in 1966.)

When Serge was 17 years old, his father suddenly died of a heart attack, at 51 years of age. This was a great blow to Serge who loved his father, with whom he had often discussed the events on the labour scene. Serge immediately blamed the unwarranted dismissal for the premature death of his father. Moreover, he was very bitter at his father's physician who had allegedly overlooked a heart ailment. He also blamed the Association of Independent Unions that had taken over the maintenance work. Having the keen sense of justice of an adolescent, Serge decided to revenge his father, whom he considered as the prototype of a victimized Quebec worker.

His asthma as a boy may have given Serge certain feelings of inadequacy, as is often the case in youngsters who are handicapped by a physical ailment. He became more of an introvert than an extrovert. He never rebelled against his parents, but he rebelled against the union rivalry which had cost his father his job, and against a society in which such injustice was possible. Rightly or wrongly, he believed that the workers of Lagrenade shoe factory and of Dominion Textile were treated unjustly, and he wanted to do something about it. At first he only distributed leaflets and copies of *La Cognée*. This was his apprenticeship, his trial period. Next they asked him to use his delicate hands to make bombs — a work demanding some skill. Then came the catastrophe: two deaths. Thereafter he stopped making bombs and took a job, hoping the world would forget all about him. But five months later the hand of the law got hold of him.

Serge has been in court more than a dozen times. He would be considered as a traitor if he told the full truth, and he actually hates to lie — a terrible conflict. He has a lawyer to protect him against the worst terror of the law, but who is going to protect him against the demoralizing effect of unsolved inner conflicts? In prison, he lacks freedom in more than one way. There is the FLQ group pressure even within the prison, telling him whether he may or may not see a priest, or a psychiatrist, or go to Mass. Who is going to liberate him?

Before Serge began to get involved with the FLQ, he planned to go to university, to study sociology and psychology. He postponed his plans in favour of terrorist activities. Four long years have passed since, during which time his personality has been lying on ice.

The Doctrinaires

There are two members of this group who strike me as particularly good examples of the doctrinaire type. I shall describe the biography of one, but the reader can be assured that the life of the other is almost exactly the same. The biography was written with the co-operation of the young man concerned, who asked that his name be withheld. We shall call him Roger.

Roger is the fourth of five children. He is not only the only delinquent but also the only separatist in the family. Born in 1947, he was brought up in a good working class family. His father earned comparatively little and during the weekends worked in a supermarket in order to better provide for the family. The children were not lacking anything essential. The father was sober, a loyal worker, understanding. His wife was a good mother and a competent housewife. Both parents were good Roman Catholics. There were only two factors which seem to have revolted the son (although they did not revolt the father): the fact that his father had to work Friday evenings and Saturdays in the supermarket, and that for many years he did not receive pay for annual holidays.

During his boyhood, Roger regularly went to a summer camp for boys. He was there eight times, but when he was 16 he preferred to stay in town. He had become a member of a gang known as *"la bande à Charlot"* which gathered in Lafontaine Park in Montreal.

In winter they met in a restaurant. The gang often took part in demonstrations (They were hired to picket certain shops), but they also committed thefts. In fact, most of the members later became delinquents. It was in this gang that Roger learned to demonstrate. One of their demonstrations was actually published in the French edition of *Maclean's* for December 1965, with Roger in the forefront. A great number of these adolescents (including the leader, Charlot) came from broken families and had dropped out of school.

Because of these exciting activities, Roger almost missed his promotion, but being of superior intelligence he caught up at the last minute and finished grade twelve. He could have gone to university but he preferred to work and become independent. At one time he worked for the garbage disposal of the city of Montreal, and used his inside knowledge to foment a strike of the garbage men. Then he found better work: he became an assistant in a biology lab. At the same time, he was an avid reader of Marxist literature and, practising what he read, never failed to take part in street demonstrations: against the Seven-Up Company, the American Consulate, the British monarchy, and so on. His behaviour at one of these demonstrations was such that the police tried to arrest him. He fought back fiercely, and was sentenced to two weeks in prison. Liberated, he was ready to take an even more active part in *Parti Pris,* where he made the acquaintance of Pierre Vallières, Serge Demers, Marcel Faulkner and others who were forming the new FLQ. He became one of its most militant members. After the explosion at Lagrenade shoe factory, fearing that the police were after him, he quit his job and found refuge in the FLQ camp at St. Alphonse. It was there that he was finally arrested.

Roger is independent in temperament, a socialist, a revolutionary and a terrorist. Even his private life is subjected to the demands of the revolution, as Lenin instructed. In the past, if a girl did not share his extremist views, he quickly exchanged her for another. As in the case with Vallières, Gagnon and a few others, violence has become an obsession for Roger. When he was sentenced, he was just 20 years old and regretted nothing. The Marxist faith had replaced the Catholic faith of his parents. He believes in class war, in civil war, and in socialism as the only system guaranteeing a better world. "A socialist system cannot be established without violence," he declares, and "terrorism is the natural consequence of the economic system of this society."

When awaiting his trial at Bordeaux prison, Roger constantly shouted separatist slogans. He does not consider himself a criminal. His only regret is the accidental death of his friend Jean Corbo, who was, in a way, his disciple. He is free from scruples. His Marxist faith justifies all means and in advance assures its believers of total absolution for anything they might do in the service of the cause.

Roger believes in the all-or-nothing principle. As we have seen, he is not the only FLQ member who sees the whole world in terms of only black and white. The Marxist slogans for him are absolute truths. Reason is everything; heart nothing. Ideas prevail over people. He will say: "The destiny of the class to which I belong is more important than my personal fate."

Like the great majority of our revolutionaries, Roger was never personally exploited. He had always had great liberty. He could have gone to university. Unlike the rest of the family, he chose alienation in its extremest form. He is another Pierre Vallières. As always, the irrational force behind his decisions is his thirst for personal liberty, which cannot be limited by the presence of a father, or an established authority. He must get what he wants. Anything or anybody standing in the way must be overthrown by the first means at hand. He violently demonstrated against the monarchy, on the Queen's Birthday, 24 May, 1965, and fought against the police who tried to establish order. Since he does not want to change himself and to adjust, he wants the world to conform to his ideas, if necessary by violence.

Such a determined man may have an extraordinary destiny. But only history will tell whether the forces he conjures up will really destroy society. Instead, he may also be destroyed in the process. As long as he is such a doctrinaire, there seem to be no other possibilities.

In October 1967, the French-Canadian writer, Claude Jasmin (soon to be known as the author of a short story, "Ethel and the

Terrorist") wrote in *Le Devoir* that since the way towards independence was now open, the time of violence had passed:

> Blind impatience will abate. The time of bombs, of thefts of arms and of outrages is over. . . . As many normal nations on this earth, we shall have a country of our own. The task will be accomplished joyously, for us and by us . . . without anger, without insults, and without hate. . . . The young generation of Quebec will be normal citizens, and one can now think of liberating the youngsters who languish in our prisons for having dared to stir us up prematurely, by way of illegality.
>
> To terminate, I would say that terrorism is a thing of the past, that Gagnon and Vallières should be liberated, as well as the other patriots of the different fronts, for our history will now develop in all liberty.

Claude Jasmin meant well, but he proved to be a false prophet.

The Fifth Wave

August 1968 - March 1969

In June 1968, a young man of a good family, aged 24, whom we shall call Pierre, failed his philosophy class in the well-known Sainte Marie junior college in Montreal. When the government refused to renew his scholarship for the following school year, he angrily decided to drop his plans to study sociology and political science, and to leave college altogether. It is true that his father had the means to pay for his studies, but Pierre did not want to be indebted to him. He wanted to be independent.

This young man had had difficulties before. He had served, with the help of the government, an apprenticeship of three years at the School of Graphic Arts in Montreal, where he had obtained a certificate as a printing operator. But then he had refused to work in this profession, claiming he found the work "stultifying." Again the government supported him with a scholarship for two years of study at the junior college, until his failure. In retaliation, one is tempted to think, Pierre became a full-time revolutionary in the summer of 1968.

He had been brought up in an affluent and permissive family and had developed a very strong sense of personal independence. Just as he found it intolerable that he should depend on his father, he found it intolerable that Quebec should depend on the federal government, or on American capital. The FLQ doctrine provided him with the means of doing something about it. Like most FLQ militants, he had first belonged to the RIN (Rassemblement pour l'indépendance nationale), and had found this association wanting. Things did not go quickly enough to his taste. Quebec once more needed a medicine which would "wake it up." Quebec needed another shot of violence.

128

Pierre Vallières' book *White Negroes of America* had a decisive influence on Pierre. He also read a lot of revolutionary literature from France, Cuba and China. But he never read Marx or Engels, and he never bought books by Marcuse. (They sold by thousands in Montreal at that time.) His reading was confined to more popular propaganda.

Pierre's knowledge of political economy is superficial. He employs the glib terminology of Pierre Vallières and Charles Gagnon. He justifies violence by saying, "We live in a violent society which can only be fought by violence." He has not worked long manually but he is convinced that all workers are exploited, and that all employers are exploiters. Like Pierre Vallières he seems to believe that the worker is good by nature and the employer or capitalist necessarily bad. This situation, as he so naively envisages it, justifies the use of equally simplistic methods to set it right. Once the good workers have the power (which they can only obtain through violence), their class enemies will vanish and a new and just society will be established without hindrance. Like most modern revolutionaries, Pierre is mainly interested in the destruction of the present society and is quite vague about the society of the future. And, like so many Quebec revolutionaries, he believes that Quebec will realize a new society which will be different from (and of course far better than) any existing socialist regime.

Pierre was brought up in an upper middle class home. His father owns a luxurious villa on the St. Lawrence River. He was a successful businessman for some years, prior to his appointment as secretary of the school commission for the district. The couple had first a girl (now married), then two boys, both intelligent, both brought up according to their social status, both with all the opportunities they could desire. Both interrupted their studies for political reasons, and both affected a proletarian way of life (and even of speech), as if they wanted to protest against their origin. At home they enjoyed the greatest liberty, and were adored by their mother.

Having dropped out of college, and not wanting to accept anything from his father, Pierre (the older of the two boys) lived in one of the worst slums in Montreal, neglected his personal appearance and was often seen surrounded by hippy-like young men. His lease was signed by a girl friend, who also paid the rent.

Pierre became the centre of a hard core of three or four terrorists. It was he who manufactured the bombs, while his comrades stole the dynamite. He probably placed the greater part of the bombs himself. Moreover, he participated in violent demonstrations. There is no doubt that he was the soul of the small group.

Our young terrorist had all the zeal of the recently converted. He says he learned bomb-making from a clandestine journal called *La Victoire*, the successor of *La Cognée*. The new bombs presented certain advantages inasmuch as they were made not only with dynamite sticks but also used Pento-mex, an even more powerful explosive. As before, the timing mechanism was an alarm clock, mostly of the Westclox type. The electricity was provided by a nine-volt battery.

La Victoire was found by the police. It was a typewritten pamphlet of ten pages. The first three were devoted to the "aims of the FLQ," as follows:

Victory over social injustice.
Victory over ignorance.
Victory over poverty.
Victory over the exploitation of man by man.
Victory over our inferior condition as a colonized people.

The author of the pamphlet gave the following picture of Quebec society:

We live under a regime of violence created by the English and the federalists. In order to preserve their interests and to continue to exploit us, they have installed, on our Quebec soil, their federal police dogs [RCMP], as well as their federal armed forces. These two elements constitute for all Quebeckers a revolver pointed at our heads. The English and the federalists are using against us a form of violence which is insulting, cruel and inhuman. Their violence is an odious blackmail existing ever since we were conquered by their arms.

One must combat violence by violence. This is why the FLQ uses the same violence against the English colonialists and their accomplices which they have themselves used against us since the conquest.

When we shall strike, the blows will be so powerful that the enemy will never recover from them.

These lines, then, were the prelude to, and the justification of, the new wave of violence that was going to follow. Seven pages of this "official organ of the FLQ" were devoted to practical matters:

How to construct a bomb.
How to fight and survive in the forest.
How to buy a weapon without a permit.
How to use a rifle MI (US) 30 semi-automatic.
Three ways of making a Molotov cocktail.

The new wave began on 8 September, 1968. The employees of the Quebec Liquor Commission were on strike at that time against the government. A bomb composed of one stick of dynamite was found and dismantled behind the liquor store at 8123 St. Denis Street in Montreal.

On 20 September, another bomb was placed, this time at the headquarters of the Black Watch, 2067 Bleury Street. This was the second time that this very English uniformed reserve unit for young people was the target of the FLQ. The bomb did not explode; it was probably meant as a warning of things to come.

Eight days later, during the night, a bomb exploded in front of another liquor outlet, at 5125 Sherbrooke Street West but there were only light property damages.

It seems that at this point the terrorists had run out of dynamite, for on 7 October they broke into an unguarded shed of Carrière Lagacé, at Chomedey, and stole about three hundred sticks of dynamite, fifty sticks of Pento-mex and about one hundred detonators. From then on, the group was able to make more powerful bombs.

On 13 October, a bomb was placed near a building of the provincial Ministry of Labour, at 355 McGill Street. Thanks to an anonymous telephone call, the police expert, Sergeant Coté, was able to dismantle the dangerous package before it could explode.

The following day, two bombs were placed. The targets were: the Renaissance Club, belonging to the Union Nationale (the government party), and the Reform Club, centre of the Liberal Party, then in opposition, headed by the same Jean Lesage who had been the target of bombs and bomb threats before. The bomb placed near the Renaissance Club was dismantled in time; the other exploded at 3 o'clock in the morning. It must be remembered that both political parties are against separatism and their leaders are considered as traitors by the FLQ.

Exactly one month later, in the night of the 13th to the 14th November, a bomb with five sticks was placed in front of the Domtar Company, at 5200 Molson Street. There was a telephone warning, and Police Sergeant Robert Coté was able to dismantle the bomb in time. The workers of the Domtar factories in East Angus, Quebec and in Windsor, Ontario were on strike at that time.

Only a day later, a bomb of eight sticks was discovered before the building of Lord & Company, at 4700 Iberville Street, and was dismantled at 1 o'clock in the morning. In this case, too, the firm was in the midst of a strike.

On 17 November, the terrorists attacked the Standard Structural Steel Company, at 5330 Pagé Street. A bomb exploded there after midnight, causing serious property damage.

Four days later, it was once more the turn of the Liquor Commission. During the night, a powerful bomb exploded in front of the liquor shop at 8360 St. Lawrence Boulevard. The show window was shattered and so were numerous windows of businesses on the opposite side of the street.

The next outrage was obviously committed to satisfy a need for publicity. On 24 November a bomb exploded at 3 a.m. at Eaton's department store. At 3 p.m. another bomb was discovered there, thanks to an anonymous telephone call. All the customers were evacuated and the bomb was dismantled. The event caused quite a flurry as the store was crowded. Although Eaton's sales per-sonnel are bilingual, in the mind of some the store is a symbol of Anglo-Saxon economic domination.

During the month of December two transportation companies became the target of the terrorist's disapproval. One was the Murray Hill Company Limited, which had the monopoly on transporting passengers from Montreal airport (a monopoly especially irritating to Montreal taxi drivers who may bring passengers to the airport, but who have to return empty). The other was Chambly Transport Company, which was in the throes of a labour conflict.

On 13 December, a bomb exploded in front of the villa of Mr. Hershon, President of Murray Hill, on Westmount Avenue, and another in front of the home of Mr. Percy Fox, Domtar executive, on Sydenham Avenue. There had been a party going on in this home; the bomb went off half an hour after the guests had left.

On the following day, three bombs were placed against the Chambly Transport Company: one before a bus garage, a second before another bus garage, at St. Hubert, and a third in front of the home of the company director. All three bombs were composed of five sticks. Only the last mentioned exploded; the others were discovered in time and removed. It was obvious that several persons were involved in the bombings, and that one of them must have had a car. (The bomb-maker never had a car and never stole one.)

The three bombs directed against Chambly Transport were pretty senseless, considering that this company was losing money at the time. The terrorists obviously wanted to support in this way the demands of the bus drivers on the South Shore, who were on strike because they wanted parity of payment with the Montreal bus drivers, the best paid in Canada.

On 17 December, 1968, the City Council of Montreal offered a reward of $10,000 for pertinent information leading to the arrest of the terrorists. On 30 December, the reward was doubled by the Quebec government. The terrorists did not waste any time in answering the challenge: on 31 December, two bombs, each of eight or nine sticks, were placed near Montreal City Hall, seat of the City Council and of Mayor Drapeau. One exploded, while the other was dismantled in time. During the same night, a bomb exploded in front of the National Revenue Building on Dorchester Boulevard. There was a telephone warning, but it came too late. This was the second bomb directed against that building. (A third one was subsequently exploded there in August 1969.)

The terrorists then seemed to direct their attention to Ottawa. Minutes before the beginning of the New Year, a bomb exploded in a letter box placed before the offices of State Secretary Gérard Pelletier. On 2 and 4 January, other bombs were discovered in letter boxes. They were taken to a field, but, owing to the cold, did not explode spontaneously.

We have already pointed out the infectiousness of acts of violence, be they bombs, hold-ups, hijacking of planes, violent demonstrations, or other manifestations of the same kind. Forty-eight bombs had been placed in Montreal since March 1968, of which less than half had exploded. The forty-ninth we will treat as a case in itself, for it had nothing to do with the FLQ.

In the evening of 6 January, 1969, about four hundred adults were taking night courses in the Ecole secondaire St. Luc, in the west end of Montreal, when a bomb exploded near the school entrance. After a close questioning of fifty students, the culprits were found in the persons of two students, one aged 16 and the other 13. They were brought before the Social Welfare Court on 8 January. The two boys admitted that they had broken into a construction shed at the University of Montreal, where they had stolen thirty-four sticks of dynamite and fifty detonators. The older boy demonstrated his technical ability by constructing a first-class time bomb in a police laboratory within fifteen minutes. He declared he had found the instructions in a Montreal tabloid. Dissatisfied with the school and wanting to protest, the two boys had decided to place a bomb of twelve sticks in the furnace room of the school building. Had the operation been successful, the school would have been out of commission for some time. There might also have been some casualties. Fortunately, when the boys tried to get to the boiler room, they heard somebody approaching, ran out of the building and threw the bomb into the snow just outside the entrance. When the bomb exploded some time later, only one stick went off, as the others were too wet. The damages were correspondingly small. The boys also admitted that they had placed another bomb on the parking lot of Trans Island Motors on Decarie Boulevard some days before, as an experiment. The bomb had exploded, but caused little damage.

The months of January and February brought a great deal of unrest to Montreal. The Stanley Gray affair* shook McGill University. The Logexpo scandal** broke out into the open, without finding its solution. The computer centre of Sir George Williams University was occupied by a group of black students on 29 January and completely wrecked on 11 February, with damage amounting to $2 million, by far the costliest single event in the wave of student unrest sweeping the world from 1967 to 1969.

It is against this atmosphere that the fifth wave of violence should be judged. It is no wonder that this wave should reach its peak in January and February 1969.

On 10 January, 1969, eleven sticks of dynamite were found in a garbage can in front of the Quebec Federation of Labour. According to FLQ tracts, the federation was led by "collaborators." Six days later, a harmless stick of dynamite was found in a mail bag.

On 21 January, the office of the Canadian Federation of Independent Associations† at 760 Crémazie Boulevard West was the target of a strong explosion. It took place at 2:15 p.m., when the building was teeming with people. A policeman was slightly hurt by the explosion. The material damages were said to be in the neighbourhood of $100,000.

Mr. Lucien Tremblay, President of the Federation, had received many threatening phone calls. He is a man who does not believe in class war, but in co-operation between workers and employers. In the language of the FLQ, he is a traitor and a collaborator.

On the same day, a padlock was smashed on a warehouse in St. Jérôme and three hundred sticks of dynamite and fifty detonators were stolen.

On 24 January, a guard found a suspicious package on the eighth

---

* Stanley Gray, a lecturer in political science, was dismissed in August of 1969 for interrupting closed meetings of the Senate and Board of Governors of the University and demanding that students be allowed to participate in the administration.
** The scandal surrounding Logexpo, an accommodation service set up for visitors to Expo 67, involved complaints of fraudulent practices.
† This association was already mentioned in connection with the fourth wave and Serge Demers.

floor of the bank of Nova Scotia Building in Montreal. He placed the package in the empty staircase, where it exploded soon afterwards. The bomb was directed to the offices of Noranda Mines and might have killed the secretary in the anteroom, had it not been removed. The Noranda Mines at that time had a dispute on their hands which involved the MIS (Mouvement intégration scolaire), a movement in favour of unilingual French schools in Quebec. A guard of the company had been particularly active for the MIS. The company had dismissed him, allegedly for unreliability, but many nationalists believed he was fired because of his convictions. All this took place more than four hundred miles from Montreal, at Matagami, where the mines are located. By exploding a bomb in front of their offices, the FLQ wanted to "warn" the company that they were being watched. The property damage amounted to $50,000. Apparently there was a telephone warning twenty minutes before the explosion but it was not taken seriously.

During the month of February there was a real escalation of bombings. One is tempted to think that the authors of this wave felt their time was running out and wanted to make good use of what remained. Here is the list of events:

8 February: a bomb (15 lbs. of dynamite) was found in front of the building of the Ministry of Labour, at 335 McGill Street, Montreal. It was the second "warning" served to the provincial Minister of Labour, and the most powerful. (The building houses the inspection services of the electrical, plumbing and construction work done in Montreal.)

10 February: At 8:58 p.m. a bomb exploded in front of the RCEME building, at 2585 Bates Street, a building which contains the technical services of the Canadian Army of the Montreal region. The guard, Maurice Cassini, 55, was fortunately not near the bomb and was only slightly injured. The property damage was in the order of several thousand dollars. The building had been the target of an FLQ explosion before, on 13 May, 1963.

11 February: Another military building became the target of the "popular" scorn. A bomb made of six sticks of dynamite plus one stick of Pento-mex, exploded at 10 p.m. in front of the Maisonneuve

Regiment building, at 695 Cathcart Street. If the guard had been near the bomb, he would have suffered O'Neill's fate. Fortunately, he was in the building and was only slightly hurt. The greatest damage was caused by the shattering of many show windows opposite the military building, in the Place Ville Marie complex.

13 February: By far the most spectacular and the most dangerous bomb outrage ever perpetrated in Quebec occurred. Shortly before 3 p.m., a bomb made of at least six sticks of dynamite and one or two sticks of Pento-mex, exploded on the main floor of the Montreal Stock Exchange. By an incredible miracle, there were no dead. Out of the three hundred persons present at the time (the majority actually French Canadians!) twenty-seven were injured more or less severely.

An official of the stock exchange later reported having received an anonymous phone call warning him that a bomb had been deposited on the main floor. But bomb scares were so frequent at that time (the police of Montreal alone received over five hundred within a month; all phony) that he did not take it seriously. The bomb outrage at the stock exchange led to still more intensive police activity. Any person carrying a parcel could henceforth be requested by the police to open it for inspection. The reward for the "head" of the terrorists was raised to $62,000.

22 February: The liberal Reform Club once more became the target of an explosion, while a wedding reception was in process. Four persons were hurt, one of them a baby.

25 February: The bookshop of the Queen's Printer, at 1182 St. Catherine West, was devastated by a bomb explosion, though nobody was hurt. The victims were all books of high quality, both in French and English, having but one defect: they were printed by Ottawa. (Moreover, the inscription over the entrance reads "Government of Canada.") It should be noted that the Queen's Printer, Mr. Roger Duhamel, is a most genuine French Canadian, and that this bookshop is about the only one which does not carry any trash.

An employee of the shop was able to give a good description of a bearded young man who had entered the shop shortly before closing time. He had examined a few books, then left without buying anything.

The bearded man was arrested in the night of 5 March, 1969, in Apartment 4, 3775 St. Dominique Street. His name: Pierre-Paul Geoffroy. Birthdate: 25 July, 1944. Marital status: single. Religion: Roman Catholic. Occupation: unemployed, ex-student. He was already known to the police for having attacked a policeman during a violent demonstration at the Seven-Up plant, in February 1968.

Pierre-Paul Geoffroy was arrested at 2 o'clock in the morning. He was alone and offered no resistance. His apartment was in a great mess. Three finished bombs were waiting. One of them was booby-trapped; it would explode if a piece of paper was removed. Since it was lying on top of ninety-seven sticks of dynamite, the whole house would have blown up, had the police not been careful.

One would expect, since the arrest took place at night, that the surroundings would have been discreetly watched during the following day, in order to bring in any witnesses and accomplices. Astonishingly, nothing of the sort was done. At 6 o'clock in the morning the radio announced Geoffroy's arrest, and a special news conference was scheduled for 7:30 a.m. by Montreal police director Robert Gilbert. Apparently he was so convinced that Geoffroy was "a lone bomber" that no precautions were taken. However, as the *Petit Journal* of 17 August, 1969 revealed, at least two friends of Geoffroy — Pierre Charrette, 26, an employee of Radio Canada (the French channel of the CBC) and Alain Allard, 22 — left Montreal in haste after hearing the news of Geoffroy's arrest. They returned only after they had the reassurance, again through the radio, that Geoffroy was supposed to have acted alone. (They have vanished since, together with another presumed accomplice, Michel Lambert.) A little later in the day, the provincial Minister of Justice imposed a blackout of news concerning Geoffroy, but it was too late.

With the arrest of P. P. Geoffroy, all bombings ceased. Within less than a year, exactly sixty bombs had been placed in Montreal alone, five in the rest of the province, and half a dozen in Ottawa. Before the court, Geoffroy pleaded guilty to thirty-one bomb charges. He also pleaded guilty to other charges, such as theft and possession of explosives. On one hand he tried to give the impression that he indeed was the lone bomber; on the other he said the outrages had been "ordered" by his cell. In fact, a number of targets obviously reflect Geoffroy's personal hatreds, so that he must have chosen some targets himself.

Pierre-Paul Geoffroy was defended by a private lawyer from his home town, Maître André Daviault. He pleaded for a mild judgement, saying that Geoffroy had seen much social injustice in his youth and had only wanted to protest against it. But Judge André Fabien was not moved. Feeling that the public had to be protected against irresponsible bombers, he gave Pierre-Paul Geoffroy a life sentence. In the audience sat the accused's younger brother, Jacques Geoffroy, and Pierre-Paul threw him the V-sign when he left the court room.

Jacques Geoffroy is just as rebellious as his brother. He too left his studies in order to overthrow the old order of things. Working for the Company of Young Canadians at St. Jérôme, forty miles northwest of Montreal, he does everything in his power to disseminate the doctrine of class war. Whether a young man of 22 who never worked manually in his life is really qualified to practise "social animation" and "education of the workers," at the expense of the Canadian taxpayer, is a moot question. Like many revolutionaries (and like his superior Pierre Renaud, a former FLQ'er), Jacques is very narcissistic, very sure of himself. He too has adopted proletarian ways, especially in his speech, and he is entirely behind his brother Pierre-Paul.

As we have seen, an important theft of dynamite was carried out in St. Jérôme on 21 January, 1969. This theft could only be accomplished with the help of somebody who, like Jacques, knew the local situation very well. A paper reported that he was actually found in possession of dynamite at that time, yet he still continued to work for the Company of Young Canadians.

The Company of Young Canadians at St. Jérôme distributed a journal entitled *Pouvoir ouvrier* (*Worker's Power*) with a clenched fist separating the two words. It is a journal wholly devoted to class hate and class war. (The bosses are called all sorts of names, such as *"les baveux."*) It resembles very much a journal I saw in Paris in the summer of 1969, which had for its title *Mort aux patrons*! (*Death to the Bosses*!). The CYC journal is not as explicit, but it actually expresses the same idea, and in the most vulgar language. The CYC also presents theatrical skits which are played to the workers as they leave the industrial plants. The skits are without literary value and are written in French-Canadian slang. It is a curious conception of education, with the teacher going below the level of his pupil in order to win him. In these skits, which were reproduced on an expensive electric government typewriter, the workers who are loyal to their employers are ridiculed, while the "fed up" and "revolted" ones who curse their work and their employers alike are made into heroes. The whole conception is extremely juvenile and superficial. Vulgarity is mistaken for a sign of strength and masculinity. It is Pierre Vallières' philosophy in a vulgarized form, but the mode of presentation derives from Mao who won his revolution by playing such skits all over China.

Since there is also a genuine Maoist group in St. Jérôme (They keep a bookstore of Maoist literature on Labelle Street), I asked them their opinion of Jacques Geoffroy and his Company of Young Canadians. The answer was: "They are but clowns."

In this connection, it is interesting to note that Pierre Vallières' fiancée, Raymonde Lorrain, also works for the Company of Young Canadians, at St. Hyacinthe, east of Montreal. She became engaged by proxy, having never seen him, solely on the strength of his book which says clearly that "social awareness" must lead to "social agitation" and from there to revolution. By financing the Company of Young Canadians in Quebec, the taxpayer was actually financing his own destruction.

To come back to Pierre-Paul Geoffroy, he too has a political fiancée. When he got to know her, she was working in the propaganda department of the Union générale des étudiants du Québec. This Union, built on the model of the extremist French student unions, was strictly unilingual, that is, French only. The students of all Quebec universities (including McGill, Bishop's, Sir George Williams) had been talked into becoming members, and the university administrations collected $70,000 per year for the Union. It is difficult to say exactly how this money was spent, but it is less difficult to guess. Student revolutionaries from Europe were invited by the Union to come and teach revolutionary tactics. The Union publicly endorsed the destruction of the Sir George Williams computer centre as justified, as it also endorsed an occupation of the department of human sciences at the University of Montreal which cost that university about $60,000 in terms of vandalism and pilfering of electrical typewriters and other equipment. The Union never paid those damages, but it is known that they paid money for the cause of Vallières and Gagnon, and probably also for Geoffroy. They probably contributed to the Black Writers Congress at McGill University (October 1968) and to the Hemispheric Conference against the war in Vietnam (November 1968). Both events are now recognized as having greatly encouraged the wave of violence (including the Stanley Gray affair) which characterized the last months of 1968 and the first months of 1969. The Union certainly financed the march on McGill University under the slogan "McGill must become French, 1969." The story of the short-lived attempt of the Union générale to "liberate" the students of Quebec would make interesting reading, but it would take us away from our main subject.

Pierre-Paul Geoffroy appealed his sentence. His brother busied himself collecting money to finance the new process, and he arranged a "Pierre-Paul Geoffroy week" with public demonstrations from the 2nd to 6th March, 1970. The week was a complete flop, despite a most impressive poster distributed at the French universities. The attempt to make a hero out of Pierre-Paul might have succeeded in the spring of 1969, but in the spring of 1970 the wind had turned, violence had lost its glamour, and with it the FLQ. A public assembly in favour of "Popaul" at the Gesu theatre was only attended by three hundred persons. It turned into a hate-filled controversy between Maoists and FLQ sympathizers, both camps shouting at each other.

Shortly after Geoffroy's arraignment, *The Gazette,* a Montreal daily, sent one of its ablest reporters, Bill Bantey, to interview Geoffroy's father. The reporter's findings were published 11 March,

1969. They were meagre enough. Pierre-Paul had been brought up to respect the established order of things. He had been educated, from the age of 12 to 17, at a boarding school, Roussin College in Montreal. Then he had gone to a bilingual high school in Ottawa, before learning his trade as a printer at the School of Graphic Arts. In short, he was a young man for whom his parents "had done everything." However, from the age of 12, in order to get the very best education, he had not lived at home, except during the holidays.

The mother had not been interviewed. Some of her acquaintances have pointed out to me how much she always admired her two sons, in whom she could find no wrong. Apparently she was proud of Pierre-Paul, because of his fortitude before the court and his refusal to name his accomplices. As to the father, he is said to have been too easy going.

Both Pierre-Paul and Jacques Geoffroy are the typical children of an affluent and permissive society. Both are rejecting their origin by adopting proletarian manners and ridiculing the value system of their parents who are so very representative of the society they want to overthrow. They want to "liberate" the workers without ever having worked with their hands themselves. Their ideology is shallow and sloganized. They project their own low frustration tolerance upon the worker whom they want to become as arrogant and demanding as they are themselves. When they speak of the violence of the present society I suspect they really mean all those restrictions and demands society makes on us (and on the workers), restrictions which the children of an affluent, permissive society will always find intolerable, whatever the economic system. They try to fashion the worker to their own image: a man ready to use any means at hand, even bombing, to get what he wants.

The Fifth Wave Peters Out

On 7 March, 1969, three days after the arrest of the presumed "lone bomber," the police of the Montreal suburb Ville St. Laurent, informed by an anonymous telephone call relayed over a radio station, found one hundred and forty-one dynamite sticks and a time bomb near a pillar supporting the elevated speedway called Metropolitan Boulevard. The device was at once dismantled. The most likely explanation of this incident is that the friends of Geoffroy wanted to get rid of an incriminating supply of explosives, while at the same time obtaining publicity.

On 2 and 3 May, two bombs exploded near the office building of the Builder's Association, causing considerable damage. At that time a part of the Quebec construction workers, led by Michel Chartrand, were on strike and, contrary to Marcel Pépin's advice, would not accept a settlement providing a 9% raise of wages for as many months. The Builder's Association had been violently attacked by the striking union, and it was pretty obvious that some of the irate strikers simply followed the example of the FLQ.

On 18 May, a bomb exploded behind the offices of the St. Jean Baptist Society in Sherbrooke, a hundred miles east of Montreal. This society had invited the Prime Minister of Canada, Pierre E. Trudeau, to its parade of 24 June. The executive of the society, as well as the Mayor of Sherbrooke, had received threatening anonymous phone calls demanding the invitation be withdrawn. Since they failed to do so, a time bomb was placed which exploded at 2 a.m., causing extensive property damage. Fearing other outrages, the committee cancelled the event altogether.

When the annual congress of the Government party of Quebec, the Union Nationale, was convening in Quebec City, some more explosions were to be expected. Sure enough, during the night of 19 June, two bombs exploded before the convention hotel, Chateau Frontenac, in Quebec City. In the evening, a third bomb exploded in the parking lot of a motel at Ste Foy, near Quebec City, where many of the delegates were staying. The authors of these outrages were never discovered, but it was noticed that a Volvo car was around each time. The car was traced to a member of the Company of Young Canadians in Montreal, but things did not go any further. There was also an explosion of gunpowder in a letter box near the convention hotel, on 20 June, caused by a bearded Montreal student, Pierre Taddeo, aged 23. Taddeo was kept thirteen days in prison, then released on bail. When he appeared before the judge, in January 1970, he was a changed man: his hair was neatly cut, his face shaved, and he wore a most conventional new "executive" suit. The judge was so impressed by the change that the culprit got a suspended sentence of two years. He willingly paid the damages. (This is the only instance of a terrorist paying for the damage he caused.)

On 7 July, Michel Chartrand's construction workers, tired of striking, vented their frustration by placing bombs near five different construction companies. There were important property damages. Finally, on 14 July, the CNTU offices (seat of the union executive opposing the strike) were destroyed during the night by a particularly powerful bomb.

Michel Chartrand, the union leader responsible for the prolongation of the strike, declared on Channel 2 that his workers were "angry" and that their actions were understandable. He put all the blame on the bosses in particular and the capitalist system in general. The police, so infallible in discovering the politically motivated terrorists, made a routine inquiry which produced no evidence.

During the same night, six incendiary devices of a new kind were found at Eaton's department store in downtown Montreal. This was the second time the store had been hit by terrorists. The devices were made with a substance which catches fire spontaneously some time after coming in contact with air or water. Two caught fire shortly after the closing of the store but the little fires were put out by the night guard. Four more devices were discovered intact during the subsequent search of the building. It is impossible to say whether the FLQ was involved in this affair or whether somebody just tried to feel important by experimenting with the new substance. Again, some papers (*La Presse*, for instance) boosted the ego of the offenders by publishing enormous headlines.

There were a few other bombs, one at Cap Rouge, near Quebec, and one in Quebec City. The first destroyed a car and was an obvious mistake, but the second hit a man who had come out publicly with the statement that the strike of the construction workers in the Quebec region was senseless and should be stopped. He paid dearly for his belief that in a democratic country everyone is entitled to express his opinion. The explosion, which occured at 2 a.m., caused a damage of $10,000, not to mention the nervous shock suffered by the victim.

During the same night, the main offices of the Industrial Acceptance Corporation, in the town of Mount Royal, were also the target of a bomb.

Ten days later, on 8 August, 1969, the offices of the provincial Minister of Labour in Ste Foy near Quebec City were damaged by a bomb explosion. One remembers that the Montreal offices of the same ministry had been "attacked" three times during the fifth wave. But this time the "warning" probably had to do with the still unsettled strike in the construction industry. Minister Bellemare himself had another theory; he expressed the opinion that the outrage was probably due to English trouble-makers. Nobody took this accusation seriously.

The terrorist acts had normally been confined to the province of Quebec, with the exception of the planned outrage on the Statue of Liberty, in 1965, the bomb in the federal Parliament (with a French-Canadian victim) in May 1966, and a few mail box bombs in January 1969 in Ottawa. On 26 August, a terrorist act directed against the federal government was committed in Vienna, Austria. A New Canadian of Hungarian origin, Kalman Losonczy, threw several Molotov cocktails into the offices of the Canadian Embassy there. The Embassy was burnt out and two Austrian employees lost their lives in the flames, while twenty-three people escaped with injuries.

Losonczy had written two letters, dated 26 August, composed in the most vulgar English. One of them was addressed to "the canadian government" (no capitals!) and began with the words: "Miserable capitalist criminals, arrogant oppressor-exploiters, stinking prostitutes and degenerate satellites of the imperialist Yankee murderers — as I told you in my letter dated 30th April 1968, I escaped from Canada, that f . . . . . English colony, where I refuse to live in destitution and misery." Losonczy called himself "a slave rebelling against the capitalist exploiter state of Canada," and he identified "the Jews and the English" as the exploiters of cheap labour.

When he had been told that his outrage had caused two deaths, he answered, "I wouldn't mind two thousand dead, if I could only revolt against Canada."

Losonczy had served in the German Wehrmacht, joining at the age of 17, and had witnessed many bestialities. Not wanting to live in communist Hungary, he came to Canada in 1951, where he experienced the usual disappointments of the newcomer. However, being intelligent, he learned English very quickly and became an accountant. He married a French-Canadian girl. Because of his unstable and irritable character, he changed jobs very often, and his wife finally decided to separate. She was divorced on 9 August, 1969.

In 1967, Losonczy, who had become a Canadian citizen during the fifties, travelled to Vienna. Not finding work, he went to the Canadian Embassy in order to get financial assistance, which was refused. He became furious, threw his Canadian passport on the floor and demanded to be released from his Canadian allegiance forthwith. Instead, he was brought back to Canada on 1 November, 1967. Following this "kidnapping," as he called it, he was obsessed by an absolutely pathological hatred of the Canadian government which was to culminate in his criminal outbreak of revenge.

Losonczy is obviously a maladjusted individual, besides being extremely obstinate, easily frustrated, and possessed by a very Hungarian type of pride. Instead of seeing the faults within himself, he held Canada responsible for all his failures. (Six months after the outrage he committed suicide.)

One may say that all this has nothing to do with the FLQ. Indeed, the procedure is different: Losonczy committed his crime in full daylight and never tried to hide his identity. On the other hand, his ideology and his "revolutionary" language seem to be borrowed from the FLQ. It is perfectly possible that without the waves of terrorism in Quebec, from 1963 to 1969, this man would not have acted as he did. Once more, we must repeat that acts of violence *are* infectious. The crimes and terrorist acts described by the mass media fascinate certain weak characters, people with a low frustration tolerance, the maladjusted who hold society responsible for their own failures, the angry young and not so young men, the permanent adolescents, and persons who, perhaps during their childhood, have been emotionally deprived or treated unjustly. Terrorist acts, just like the hold-ups, are contagious, even if the number of persons susceptible of catching the disease is very limited.

Pierre Vallières has said that even in quiet times "spectacular actions" have to be carried out from time to time, in order to keep the pot boiling. One of these actions occurred in the night of 28 September, 1969 when the residence of Mayor Drapeau was dynamited at 4 a.m. The Mayor was not at home but his family got quite a shock. The house did not fall in but was later declared to be beyond repair. Mayor Drapeau is certainly the most dynamic and the most honest Mayor Montreal has had for a long time, but according to the FLQ publications he sided too much with the English, was not anti-American, and did not discriminate against capitalism. He had protested against General de Gaulle's meddling in Quebec affairs in 1967, telling him that Quebec had been able to manage without France for over two hundred years and did not need her support now. In his *White Negroes,* Pierre Vallières had placed Drapeau on a level with Hitler.

On 20 November, there were two bombs: one before the residence of Mr. Barone, at St. Leonard near Montreal, and another at Loyola College where the dismissal of an extremist foreign professor had led to much student agitation. Mr. Barone is of Italian origin and a successful building contractor. He had already been "bomb-warned" on 1 September, 1964. Since then, he had come out strongly against the unilingual school system forced upon St. Leonard. His residence was to be the target of the third bomb on 8 December, 1969.

In November, there were a few more bomb outrages of minor importance, such as the destruction of a greenhouse on McGill campus. On 22 December, somebody went back to the methods of 1963 by placing a time bomb in a mail box. The package was cleared with the rest of the mail and put inside a van. The device exploded some time later, just when the driver, a French Canadian, had left the vehicle in order to empty another mail box. Had the explosion occurred while he was driving, he or somebody else might have been killed.

However, the second half of 1969 and the beginning of 1970 became a time of reassessment rather than action. The terrorism of bombs had yielded less than the FLQ had expected. Even the paroxysm due to Geoffroy had not helped. Neither the authorities, nor the judges, nor the political parties, nor the great majority of the people showed any signs of weakening. René Lévesque, founder of the separatist Parti québecois had come out several times against the "senseless" bombings. The overwhelming majority of the workers remained sceptical. The public in general did not like the sound of explosions, still less did they relish "patriotic" hold-ups. The FLQ, besides not having the success they had expected, had also lost a few "patriots." And finally, about a dozen members were in prison, hoping to be granted parole, and parole would, of course, be refused if the bombs continued to explode. Obviously, the structure and the methods had to be overhauled. Puerile acts had to be replaced by more professional coups. The attention was to be turned to social disturbance and agitation, the radicalization of labour conflicts, the infiltration by the FLQ of workers' and citizens' committees. No occasion should be missed to demonstrate against the authorities, be it in favour of Vallières, Gagnon or Geoffroy, or against "fascism," "federalism" and "capitalism." The FLQ would remain clandestine as before, but would take part in authorized or at least public demonstrations where the real agents could hide in the mass of the demonstrators. There were also attempts to link up with Black Power, with student revolutionaries abroad, with "liberation movements" elsewhere. Charles Gagnon publicly supported the Arab terrorists working for the "liberation of Palestine," a move which makes the FLQ a potentially anti-Semitic movement.

The present political climate in Quebec is favourable for every kind of subversion and a good ground for agitators of any sort. The numerous and often senseless labour conflicts, most of them very bitter and very prolonged, the innumerable political squabbles, the many dissensions among and within the parties, the Latin emotionality of the French Canadians, the high rate of unemployment fostered by periodic labour violence, are all factors creating an atmosphere of political and social unrest in which everyone can blame the authorities or "the system" for his own failures. But what contributes even more to this atmosphere is the widespread contempt of the law. Nothing could help the revolutionaries more than the tendency, so prevalent amongst the young generation, to take the law into their own hands and to believe that the end justifies the means. This is why revolutionaries of every sort will foster this mentality not only among the young but also among the workers.

A good insight into the future programme of the Quebec extremists can be obtained from a secret manifesto of the Front de libération populaire. The FLP is the FLQ without bombs, and the author of the manifesto (which was at first only reproduced in twenty copies) was probably a former FLQ member who later became a worker for the Company of Young Canadians in Montreal and now plays a leading role in the FLP, together with Stanley Gray.

The manifesto outlines the common strategy which will be followed by the FLP, the Liberation of Taxi movement (MLT), the movement for unilingual schools (MIS), the committee Gagnon-Vallières, the citizens' committees, and some labour unions. All these groups, while not losing their individual characteristics, are invited to work together for a common strategic goal: the violent overthrow of the present political and economic system in Quebec. This "war of liberation" is presumed to take place in three stages:

  1. The first phase will be social agitation, radicalization of labour

conflicts. This phase will be mainly political, but this will not exclude violent acts, urban guerilla activities, and so on.

2. Once "the popular anger becomes generalized," the unions will also become revolutionary. In every factory, every labour union, every university, every CEGEP, even in every quarter of the town, professional revolutionaries will lead the people under their jurisdiction.

3. The final phase, leading to "the destruction of the bourgeois order of things," will be of a military order: armed occupation of factories, universities, schools, public services, government buildings and of the whole territory.

The manifesto demands that the militants should do their revolutionary homework by studying revolutionary tactics and acquiring ideological theory and training.

On the plane of action, "agitation and contestation must become permanent features, unmasking, demystifying and weakening the mechanism of the system which keeps the workers and the students in stifling slavery."

Such action "will naturally lead to violence and illegality." But this is "absolutely normal," for "legality is nothing but the judiciary justification, imposed by force, of the 'right' of the exploiters to dominate and exploit 90% of their fellow men." Therefore, "one must not be afraid of illegality."

The author also recalls security measures such as: Never keep a list of militants. Never discuss anything by phone. By all means avoid "the mortal decapitation in case of a heavy blow."* Since the war against capitalism and imperialism cannot be won openly, clandestinity will more and more become a necessity.

In a final paragraph, the author answers certain criticisms concerning the FLQ bombings:

Some say that the bombs were not warranted by any strategic necessity and that they invited repression and did not damage the economy seriously. Yet bombs play their part in the strategy just

---

* Obviously an allusion to the arrests of Gagnon and Vallières, which had hurt the FLQ very much.

as do the demonstrations of the MLT and the FLP. All aim at the radicalization of the political agitation. They develop an increasing class consciousness in the exploited ones. For the moment, the significance of the bombs is political rather than material. Their basic aim is not to destroy the economic basis of the system, but to endeavour to radicalize the conflicts produced by the inner contradictions of the system itself up to the point of no-return, to the point of the break-down, of the final confrontation. The decisive attacks on the economic foundations of the regime will come at a later stage of the fight. There is so much to denounce in the system, so much to contest and to destroy, that we should not waste our energies to make the FLQ a convenient scapegoat for everyone. One should not forget that all the Quebec revolutionaries, by their action and their determination, have made the FLQ possible. And the FLQ will last as long as there are in Quebec revolutionaries determined to win.

This truly frightful document reflects the thinking of the hard core of the FLQ. It is in no way an official programme and I have been told that it was actually put in cold storage in view of the provincial elections of the spring of 1970, with the idea of first getting as much power as possible by legal action. But if legal political activity, including social agitation, would not lead to a paralysis of the system, illegality would become mandatory and the programme would be implemented.

The FLQ Degenerates (1970)

While there were no bombings until May, the pot of revolution had to be kept boiling in other ways. Pierre-Paul Geoffroy had appealed his sentence. This was done, so his friends said, not so much because there was anything to be gained, but "for purposes of political propaganda." Indeed, it is one of the rules of revolutionary tactics to constantly harass the courts with demands, appeals and complaints in order to gain publicity. Already Hitler, in his *Mein Kampf*, had said that nothing worse could befall a revolutionary movement than to be forgotten.

Another way of keeping the pot boiling was to invite the German-French revolutionary Cohn-Bendit to Canada, where he was interviewed on the English network of the CBC, after having been received at the Montreal airport by Stanley Gray and Bernard Mataigne of the Front de libération populaire. The interview itself was extremely revealing. Cohn-Bendit, whose role in Europe is practically finished, instead of answering the questions put to him, gave a display of narcissistic self-importance such as has rarely been seen on television. He behaved as if he was graciously granting an audience, and spoke only about himself. Having pocketed a big fee, he left for Germany.

Geoffroy's appeal was used to gain publicity. His brother Jacques Geoffroy, formerly of the Company of Young Canadians and a violent revolutionary himself, launched a subscription and sympathy campaign: "A group of friends and sympathizers of the political prisoner [*sic*] in St. Jérôme have undertaken to collect funds to aid Geoffroy, who comes from this Laurentian town. The contributions should be addressed to Mr. Jacques Geoffroy, 365 Melançon, St. Jérôme." The appeal was launched at the beginning of February.

A month later, about $550 had been collected. The week from the 2nd to the 6th of March was designated as "Pierre-Paul Geoffroy Week," and demonstrations were scheduled to take place in Montreal, just at the moment when the appeal was expected to come up before the court. Jacques Geoffroy published a pamphlet which was widely distributed on the campus of the French universities of Montreal, together with a drawing of Pierre-Paul which made him look like a young Ché Guevara. Among other things, the pamphlet said, "The FLQ is an organized and determined movement, grouping people who have decided to change the social and economic system which at present stifles the great majority of the Quebec population. Terrorism is, in fact, a lucid taking of sides in favour of violent action. The terrorists consider this action necessary, if we really intend to overthrow the exaggerated power of those who dominate us, and to give the power to the people. The judge who sentenced Geoffroy gave him such a high sentence because he only considered the number of bombs and the places where they were placed, instead of taking into account the material damages and the [non-lethal] consequences for persons present during the explosions. Geoffroy had identified the enemy; he fought him on his own ground." Therefore the judge wanted to stipulate an example "so that nobody else should touch the master." The authors of the pamphlet assured the readers that they did not want to "take up the actions of Geoffroy," that "terrorism was only one of several possibilities," but that they wanted their friends "to become more radical in solidarity."

The Hudon II Group

Meanwhile, towards the end of 1969, a new clandestine group was forming. It consisted of three cells whose members knew each other despite the rules laid down by Pierre Vallières. The first group, led by Robert Hudon, an ex-terrorist of the second wave, out on parole, was called the "action group." It was to specialize in hold-ups. Another group directed by Robert's older brother, Gabriel Hudon, the bomb-maker of the first wave, out on parole, specialized in research. It spied out suitable locations for the hold-ups and planned the actions. A third group, led by a journalist, J.D., already involved in the Schirm group, specialized in training for hold-ups and presumably kidnapping. It goes without saying that the action group provided the money for the two others. The groups also kept a file on different persons. The filing cards were later found at Lac Larouche near Chicoutimi.

The soldiers of the action group were Marc-André Lavoie, alias Gagné, and Pierre Demers. The group was extremely active: it committed no less than twenty-one hold-ups before the first arrest. Almost half of these were the work of Marc-André alone. About a dozen were carried out in common. In the fall the action group had made the acquaintance of a 17-year-old boy whose parents owned a camp at St. Calixte. Thanks to this friendship, the group, in December, took a two-week holiday there, during which they mainly watched TV. At the end of the two weeks, the owner asked them to leave. Marc-André was a drop-out of the Philosophy Department at the University of Quebec, in Montreal.

At one time, shortly before he joined the FLQ, Marc-André was Vice-President of a student union and was so busy "with student unionism" (*syndicalisme étudiant*, a term imported from France) that he found no time for studying. He was also spending a lot of money. He took part in the violent demonstration on St. James Street. His way of life and the absolute recklessness he displayed during the hold-ups suggest that he must have been in a constant state of euphoria and elation which made him overlook any dangers. Before the court, Marc-André claimed he was frustrated because the government had refused him a bursary (probably because nobody had confidence in his desire to study). So it seems that, very much like Pierre-Paul Geoffroy, he felt the need to hit back. He had never committed a theft before joining the group, let alone a hold-up. But once drugged with revolutionary slogans, he developed such a frenzy for hold-ups and such daring that he even astonished his partners. At times he committed one hold-up per day! The money went to the chief, Robert Hudon, who distributed it among the three groups. Within a little over a month over $24,000 was "collected." The victims were ten pharmacies (nine of them French-Canadian), a grocery, a post office, a licence bureau, a garage, and five banks. His biggest haul was from the Caisse populaire of St. Vincent de Paul, right under the nose of the guard standing on top of the prison walls of the adjacent St. Vincent de Paul penitentiary, where he was later incarcerated. He would have been satisfied with $500 (His gun was not loaded), but they gave him $5,500. His last successful hold-up took place in Ontario. Nobody knows why he chose that location.

Seeing that he got very little of the proceeds, while Robert Hudon bought beautiful furniture, rented a nice apartment and indulged in expensive drinks, Marc-André felt exploited, and finally, after a violent quarrel, separated from the group. He was arrested on 12 March, 1970, while trying to commit a theft. He pleaded guilty and was released on bail which was set at $950. However, after a second appearance before the judge, he was kept in prison. An investigation revealed the full story.

On 8 June, 1970, Marc-André Lavoie (Gagné), having pleaded guilty, was sentenced to twenty-five years in penitentiary for a number of hold-ups. He did not reveal the names of his partners. In sentencing him, the judge followed the instructions for heavier sentences in cases of armed robberies.

The Hudon II group not only perpetrated hold-ups, they also tried the first kidnapping in the history of the FLQ. The plan was apparently elaborated in detail by the research group headed by J.D. The kidnapping was probably to take place on 23 February, 1970, Charles Gagnon's birthday, and the intended victim was none other than Charles Gagnon himself. The whole project sounds like a farce, but it was serious enough. A small truck had been hired for the purpose. For good measure, Mr. Lemieux, Mr. Larue-Langlois and Stanley Gray were also to be kidnapped. In this first kidnap attempt, everything went wrong. Apparently the leader, Robert Hudon, was too drunk to direct the operation. Moreover, Charles had been warned, and stayed away. Nor did he later turn up at his birthday party at "Le Patriote" where his admirers, including Larue-Langlois, Lemieux, Jacques Geoffroy, Geoffroy's father and sister were assembled. Only a message came: Charles was sick.

The reason why the Hudon group wanted to kidnap Charles

Gagnon was because they reproached him for having spoken in the name of the FLQ on the French TV network. They wanted to teach him a lesson and, by means of torture if necessary, make him sign a statement that he would henceforth refrain from making unauthorized statements and from monopolizing the FLQ spotlight. Larue-Langlois and Lemieux were to get the same treatment.

But a still better joke was to come. The very haunt of the FLQ patriots and their sympathizers, the restaurant with bar and cabaret "Le Patriote," was held up by an FLQ militant on a Saturday evening. The manager, Yves Blais, had to hand over $660 to the armed FLQ bandit, whose comrades were actually sitting in the restaurant, sipping whisky and looking at a show which they later described as boring. The reason for this hold-up was, apparently, that FLQ money had been invested in "Le Patriote," but the members of the group found that it had been getting more than its patriotic share and wanted some of it back!

After his arrest, Marc-André was replaced by another terrorist. In the meantime, a new group had been formed in the Lake St. Jean region, and the two groups pooled their resources. Yet the end of the Hudon group was at hand. Their last hold-up took place on 25 May, at St. Calixte, thirty-five miles north of Montreal. The following report is based on a story by Gérard Asselin in the *Petit Journal* of Montreal (7 June, 1970):

The plan had probably been worked out in the Lake St. Jean district. The region of St. Calixte was chosen because both Hudons knew the surroundings well. The research group had done its groundwork, spying out the locale. Four men took part in the hold-up: Gabriel Hudon as supervisor, Robert Hudon as leader of the action, Robert Tremblay and Jean Lessard (both from Lake St. Jean) as henchmen.

Gabriel used his own car to drive the party towards St. Calixte. The passengers disembarked at a forest not far from the village. Gabriel drove to St. Jérôme where he parked his car. He took a taxi and let himself drive back towards St. Calixte. Passing the forest, he told the taxi driver to stop. Robert Hudon emerged from the trees, masked and fully armed and ordered the taxi driver to beat it. This happened two miles from the village. Gabriel drove the taxi there, parked in front of the Caisse populaire, and the armed and masked men tried to get into the bank. Since it was not yet 10 o'clock, the door was locked, but Robert opened it with a few shots of his powerful Browning 45. In less than a minute, the four men were in possession of over $3,000.

The revolver shots had attracted the attention of the mayor, who seized a rifle, ran up to his balcony, and began shooting at the hold-up men rushing back to their taxi. One bullet passed an inch by Robert Hudon's head. The four made off with great speed. Some miles away, they abandoned the bullet-marked car and took to the forest trails which they knew so well and which led them finally to St. Hippolyte. The night was passed in a shed. The following morning, Gabriel returned to St. Jérôme to retrieve his car. To his relief, no policeman was to be seen anywhere.

The others went back to the Lake St. Jean district where they divided the loot. As usual, part of the money went to the cell which, as can now be presumed, "studied" kidnappings.

Three days later, all four men were arrested. Robert Hudon admitted to this last hold-up. There was a strong suspicion that a well-known FLQ leader had given them away in retaliation for the abortive kidnap attempt. At any rate, the group had acted too independently, was strongly opposed to Vallières and Gagnon and thus had become a liability for the movement. Despite the fact that Robert Hudon had failed in life and only excelled as a bandit, he still ranks as a "patriot" and a "political" prisoner in the official FLQ nomenclature. One day, when we know the full story of the dissensions and quarrels within the FLQ, we will have cause to marvel at the fact that, for the outsider, the FLQ always manages to keep up the pretence of an ideological front united by a common ideal. The reality is quite different.

Gagnon Seeks Support in English Canada

As usual, revolutionary agitation began to pick up in the spring. While the Hudon II group was committing its hold-ups, Charles Gagnon and Jacques Larue-Langlois, manager of the Committee in Aid of the Vallières-Gagnon Group (now also called the Aid Committee for Political Prisoners) toured campuses in English-speaking Canada. Speaking before students of Waterloo University in Ontario on 25 March, Larue-Langlois said: "The main objective of liberation struggles is to give all power to the people. This means that the basic units of society, workers, students, and other proletarians would administer themselves." This, of course, is a polite description of the dictatorship of the proletariat, to which all other classes of society would be subjected.

He also justified the FLQ outrages by pointing out their publicity value. FLQ press releases would be ignored by the press, he said, whereas a bombing of the Montreal Stock Exchange would get front-page treatment. Moreover, such outrages helped the workers "to identify the enemy."

Then Gagnon declared, "The war in Quebec is real. It's just beginning, but it will grow."

A Hot May

And grow it did. In May and June, events followed at an even greater pace. The week 5-12 May was designated "Operation Vallières Week," and was highlighted with public speeches by Gagnon, non-authorized street demonstrations, and meetings among representatives of the FLQ, union representatives and workers' committees. The junior colleges (CEGEP) with their highly inflammable student material were also mobilized. As to the street demonstration planned for 12 May, 1970 Gagnon declared: "We had not asked for a permit as a matter of principle." The police dispersed the demonstrators to the shouts of "*Chiens!*" and "Repression!" Gagnon later declared that the week organized by the Aid Committee, in order to "demand the unconditional liberation of Pierre Vallières as well as of all the other political prisoners," had been a complete success.

Yet ten days later, Vallières was still in prison. He then began his second hunger strike, a fact which was duly publicized. Six days later, on 26 May, he was out on bail, awaiting the outcome of his appeal against a thirty-months' sentence for his involvement in the Lagrenade case. He had been in jail since the end of September

1966, had been condemned to life, and then (in a new trial) to thirty months. The appeal was scheduled for September 1970, and then for November. Not everybody was happy about this liberation. The Maoist journal, *Le Patriote rouge*, declared that Vallières and Gagnon were but "fascists of the left." But others celebrated the release of Vallières with fireworks of a special kind.

Indeed, within one month, beginning with 24 May and ending 24 June, thirteen bombs exploded in Montreal, another in Tracy, Quebec, and a fifteenth in Ottawa. Here is the list:

24 May: Canadian General Electric
28 May: Queen Mary Veterans' Hospital
31 May: Financial Collection Agency
           Home of Peter Bronfman in Westmount
           An empty home in Westmount
           Home of Mr. Nobbs, Westmount
           Home of Mr. McCuaig, Westmount
 5 June: Canadian Club, Montreal; mainly damaging a medical
           centre nearby
16 June: University of McGill campus
18 June: Postal substation in Longueuil
19 June: Private home in Outremont
24 June: Postal station in Montreal.
           Bomb at a building of the Ministry of Defence, Ottawa

This last bomb killed a French-Canadian mother, Mrs. Jeanne d'Arc Saint-Germain, aged 50. The FLQ had scored another French Canadian. The lady was working at the telecommunications centre of the National Defence Ministry. Again it was difficult to see how the killing of a French Canadian could help the cause of Quebec. The terrorists must have wondered too, for they stopped their bombing campaign right there.

Apart from the fifteen bombs which exploded, a few more were found in time to be dismantled: two near the IBM Canada Ltd. offices, not far from the Montreal airport, a third at the research laboratories of Domtar Chemicals Ltd., and about ten others, in different places, all in the month of June.

A Cell is Nipped in the Bud

While bombs were exploding in Westmount, another group of terrorists, who obviously worked on their own, committed a number of hold-ups. The most daring was the hold-up of the social centre of the University of Montreal, where they took over $58,000. Here it could hardly be said they were taking money from the rich to make a levy off the capitalists. They were taking it from students. It can safely be assumed that they got a tip from a student about the money being deposited at the time. In order to distract the attention of the police, they set two bombs to go off shortly before the hold-up was to take place.

The Minister of Justice for Quebec had offered a reward of $50,000 to anyone providing a decisive tip as to the identity of the bombers, and the group were promptly given away. They were all arrested in a summer house they had rented at Prévost, thirty-five miles north of Montreal. There the police discovered arms, hoods, a Chinese timing device, three thousand circulars calling for "a revolution for Quebec workers," over $20,000 and a lot of dynamite and ammunition. Another larger cache of dynamite was found stored away under a trap in a house at Duvernay, whose owner had no idea he was living dangerously. The cache was the work of his son, who lived somewhere else. Six persons were arrested: André Roy, 23, who called himself an unemployed taxi driver; his wife Nicole, 26, who claimed to have had no inkling of what her husband did and where the money came from; Pierre Carrier, 30, "unemployed"; his girl friend Maude Martin, 26, script girl at Radio Canada; Claude Morency, 19, "unemployed"; and François Lanctot, 21, labourer. A little later, two more accomplices were arrested.

The two women were released without charges being laid. As to the men, they were held after a preliminary inquiry. On advice of Mr. Lemieux they pleaded Not guilty and chose trial by jury. The lawyer did everything to make the selection of this jury as difficult and as lengthy as possible.

This new group had several unique qualities: it consisted of workers only — and they were eight, which is twice as many as an FLQ cell should number. There was no proper leader, nor did they seem to receive any orders from some coordinating brain above.

In June 1970, the police got hold of two well-armed men driving a truck. The obvious conclusion was that they were on the way to some hold-up, but the truth was different. They were actually on the way to kidnap the Israeli consul! One of the would-be kidnappers was none other than François' older brother who was not yet arrested at the time. Jacques Lanctot, 25, came before the judge for possession of offensive weapons. Unfortunately he was granted bail and disappeared. Had he been held in custody, the later kidnappings which rocked Canada in October might never have materialized. The other driver was Guy Marcil, who was also released on bail, but who was arrested later when their kidnapping plot (Operation Marcil-Lanctot) came to light. (Once again he was released on bail!)

During the search at the Prévost chalet, the police indeed found a detailed plan to kidnap the Consul General of the United States in Montreal, Mr. Harrison Burgess. Even the communiqué to be given to the press was already run off on a stolen Gestetner machine. It read as follows:

The disgusting representative of the USA in Quebec, the Consul Harrison W. Burgess, is in the hands of the FLQ. These are the conditions on which the life of Consul Burgess depends:

1. Liberation of the political prisoners: Serge Demers, Marcel Faulkner, Charles Gagnon, Pierre-Paul Geoffroy, Edmond Guénette, Gérard Laquerre, Robert Lévesque, Pierre Marcil, Rhéal Matthieu, François Schirm, Claude Simard, Pierre Vallières.

2. Reinstatement of the revolutionary Lapalme workers by the federal government solely on the conditions of the revolutionary Lapalme workers.

3. Voluntary tax of $500,000 in gold ingots.

The following precautions are to be taken by the established authorities in order to maintain Consul Burgess in good health. The established authorities must see to it that:

1. All communiqués handed out by the FLQ be fully broadcast on radio and television and be published in all major newspapers of Quebec.

2. The repressive police forces will not commit the monstrous error of investigations, searches, arrests or any other tricks aiming at foiling the success of this FLQ action. All these will threaten the life of Consul Burgess.

Moreover, the established authorities must carefully observe the following rules:

1. All the political prisoners are to be liberated at once and transported immediately to the international airport of Montreal.

2. A room will be put at their disposal in order that they may communicate with their lawyers and meet anyone they want to see.

3. The prisoners must not be submitted to any harm, duress or torture.

4. They must be given one hour of television on the state network, in the evening.

5. The population is to be asked to meet the patriotic prisoners and see them off.

6. The political prisoners are to be free to leave Quebec, or to refuse to do so; in other words, they have the right to differ, but must explain their choice to the population.

7. A plane is to be put at their disposition for their transportation to Cuba, and they are to be accompanied by their respective lawyers, and by at least two journalists chosen by the Board of Editors of Québec-Presse.

8. The voluntary tax of $500,000 is to be verified before the TV cameras before being placed on the plane.

9. The return of these legal advisers and the journalists is to be assured, from Cuba to Montreal.

All these conditions are to be met within twenty-four hours from the broadcasting of the present communiqué. All conditions are irrevocable, and the life of Consul Burgess depends only on the compliance of the authorities.

The communiqué then said that Mr. Burgess would be released after the return from Cuba of the legal advisers and after the other demands were met. Then the communiqué explained the action in a world context:

By the kidnapping of Consul Burgess the FLQ wants to stress its revolutionary solidarity with all those countries which fight against the economic, social and cultural domination of the Americans in the world. This means unconditional support of the movements in Latin America and Palestine, support of the American blacks and of all the peoples of Africa and Asia who work for their liberation.

The FLQ thus aligns itself with the Cuban stand which vigorously denounces American imperialism and which promises to support all those fighting against that hegemony. The political prisoners will surely be able to benefit from the extraordinary experience of the Cubans, whom we want to thank in advance for the concern they will show to our comrades the political prisoners.

> Long live the Cuban People!
> Long live Fidel!
> Long live the Cuban revolution!

This very enlightening document, written of course without any contact with Cuban officials, necessarily led to a tightening of precautions on the part of American officials. But what we find incredible is that the official representatives of other countries did not receive at least a set of rules aimed at preventing kidnapping attempts. This was obviously not the case, for experience has shown that the potential objects of further kidnapping plots continued to live in a carefree, relaxed atmosphere.

The communiqué was accompanied by a manifesto, to be read on all radio stations and to be published in all major journals. In this manifesto, the anonymous authors posed as the defenders of the working class of Quebec.

While the activities of this last cell were being exposed, Dr. Serge Mongeau and other sympathizers launched a subscription campaign in favour of the "political prisoners." The objective was $50,000, "for the defence of all Quebeckers detained on charges arising from their opinions or alleged opinions, or from their political stand, or acts based on these opinions or declarations." The appeal for funds was signed, among others, by Larue-Langlois, and by the poet Gaston Miron ("the spiritual father of the FLQ," according to Vallières.) The sum of $50,000 was small compared with the over

$100,000 accruing from FLQ hold-ups within six months. It was expected that labour unions and especially teachers' unions would contribute heavily to this "Movement for the defence of the political prisoners." Nor was the question even considered whether the "political prisoners" really could or would be helped in this way, especially as the National Parole Board, in order to safeguard the equality of all before the law, refuses to deal with lawyers representing individual prisoners.

As always after the destruction of an action group, the front was relatively quiet until October 1970, when Canada was shocked to learn that "it could happen here." The FLQ once more was imitating foreign models. From September 1969 to 31 July, 1970 thirteen innocent people, mostly foreign diplomats, had been abducted in Central and South America. Two of them were assassinated, one escaped, the others were traded for political prisoners who had never been before a court. Now it was Quebec's turn.

The abduction of Mr. James Cross, British Trade Commissioner in Montreal, on 5 October, and the abduction of Mr. Pierre Laporte, Minister of Labour and Immigration, on 10 October, shook the population of Quebec, of Canada and the whole world. The conditions for their release were virtually the same as those mentioned in the document found on June 21 which implied that there was a connection. The police soon concluded that Jacques Lanctot, 25, a brother of the François Lanctot arrested at Prévost, must have directed the abduction of Mr. Cross.

This is a summary of the events:

5 October, 8.15: Four armed individuals rang at the door of 1297 Redpath Crescent, Montreal, and were admitted inside by the maid. They took Mr. James R. Cross out of his room and drove away with him.

Shortly before noon, "Communiqué No. 1" was found at a University of Quebec building in Montreal, a communiqué in which the FLQ outlined the conditions for the release of their hostage. The "established authorities" were told to comply with the following conditions:

1. Publish an FLQ manifesto in all the newspapers and on French TV.

2. Liberate the consenting "political prisoners."

3. Transport freed prisoners by plane to Cuba or Algeria.

4. Reinstate the Lapalme workers in their former job with the Montreal Post Office.

5. Pay a ransom of $500,000 in gold ingots.

6. Give away the name of the informer responsible for the recent arrests.

7. Cease all police activities, searches, and so on, in connection with the kidnapping.

6 October: Two more communiqués were received. They betrayed great nervousness and impatience and threatened to "liquidate" the British diplomat.

7 October: A fourth communiqué was sent to a radio station, demanding that the manifesto be read on TV the very same day. Foreign Minister Mitchell Sharp declared on TV that the demands of the kidnappers were unreasonable, but declared his readiness to negotiate.

8 October: For "humanitarian reasons," the manifesto was read on the French TV. Communiqué No. 5 again demanded that all police activities must cease.

9 October: Communiqués No. 6 and 7 fixed a new deadline. The authorities were given twenty-four hours to comply.

During this time, three letters by Mr. Cross to his wife came through.

The impatience of the kidnappers was reflected in the fact that they set unrealistic deadlines. However, from their communiqués it became clear that they would settle for far less than their original demands and that they probably would have been satisfied with obtaining the liberation of from six to eight of their comrades who were in prison, Geoffroy being the most important. But then a new incident jeopardized everything.

Obviously dissatisfied with the way things were going and with the apparent softening of the kidnappers of Mr. Cross, another group which called itself the "Chénier cell," staged a second kidnapping, taking Mr. Pierre Laporte, Minister of Labour of the Quebec Government away from his home in St. Lambert, situated on the south shore of the St. Lawrence River. This group immediately let it be known through a private radio station that they demanded the integral fulfilment of all seven points.

The federal and provincial governments declared again that they could not accede to these demands. If they did, this would mean that other kidnappings would take place each time some FLQ member had to go to prison. Opinion polls showed that the great majority of the population shared this view. Mr. René Lévesque, however, launched an appeal, signed by numerous personalities, that a number of prisoners be liberated and sent to Cuba, together with the kidnappers. The Quebec government appointed a lawyer to negotiate with both groups.

The demands were obviously made by young people who did not understand how a government functions. The deadlines, several times extended, were ridiculously short. Of the twenty-three prisoners mentioned, three were not even in jail, a fourth was seriously ill, a fifth a mental patient. A sixth is not a Canadian citizen and could have been deported long ago. Another eight would be eligible for parole. It was obvious that the abductors only knew a few of the prisoners they wanted to liberate. They had no assurance whether Cuba or Algeria would accept them at all. As to the $500,000, any decent country would, of course, return the gold immediately. As to the Lapalme workers, the abductors actually asked that four hundred family fathers be dismissed illegally in order to install those Lapalme "revolutionary workers" who had disrupted the Montreal mail service in February and had refused to be engaged on the same terms as the other postal workers all over Canada. Of the seven points, only the liberation of some prisoners and the publication of the manifesto could be taken seriously. By demanding the impossible, the FLQ abductors actually hurt their own cause. They virtually wanted the authorities to abdicate.

Right after the abduction of Laporte, I wrote a letter to *Le Devoir* in which I said:

The two crimes which have been committed and are still perpetrated have divided the Quebec people more than any other issue has ever done. Confronted with those deeds of violence, every man and woman in this province has to stand up and be counted. There can be no ambiguity here, no neutrality, no whitewashing. Either you are in one camp or in the other, for or against. As in the past, silence will be taken by the FLQ as tacit approval, sympathy as loud applause.

(The letter was never published.)

The well-known FLQ people did not say a word. For them Cross and Laporte were members of the Establishment — not worth a thought. Since anything is moral which helps the cause, the abduction was in order. But nobody would have thought it possible that the top union heads of Montreal would make political capital of a crime. Everybody was astonished to read the following statement: "The Central Committee of National Trade Unions in Montreal, confronted with an attempt, on the part of the authorities, to sow panic in the population of Quebec, wants to reaffirm its conviction that the FLQ will never attack the wage-earners, but rather the ruling minority which is the cause of all the present ills in Quebec." At the same time, the Central Committee made it known that it supported the manifesto of the abductors! Those Quebec labour leaders who, without a mandate from their members, obviously endorse FLQ policy because they think that everything that diminishes the power of the lawful government is grist to their mill, are playing a dangerous game. The German industrialists who supported Hitler financially because of his anti-communist stand played the same game and lost.

In order to boost the morale of the FLQ sympathizers, there was also a rally, attended by 2,000 students, in support of the manifesto and the demands of the FLQ abductors, with Lemieux, Chartrand, Vallières and Gagnon speaking. This at a time when every citizen was deeply ashamed of what had happened!

In the meantime, Laporte was kept in a bungalow not far away from his home. Since the colour and shape of the car used for the abduction was known, and since it was obvious that the abductors must have remained in the vicinity, the obvious thing to do was to look systematically into every garage in the three communities. This would have taken a hundred men less than a day and would have led to the quick discovery of the hiding place. Nothing of the sort was done.

Pierre Laporte was killed one week after being abducted, on Saturday, 17 October. The sadistic manner of the killing suggests that the killer was a pervert who may also have been under the influence of drugs.

Following an anonymous telephone call, Laporte's body was found in the trunk of the car which had been used for the abduction, near the heavily guarded airport of St. Hubert, and now the police, searching systematically, soon discovered the place where he had been kept captive.

The identity of two suspects was soon established: one was Paul Rose, 27, a part time teacher (!) who was known to surround himself with young hippies and drug addicts; the other was Marc Carbonneau, 37, who had played a conspicuous role in the violent demonstrations against Murray Hill earlier in the year. (Suspicion later swung to Jacques Rose rather than Carbonneau).

The assassination of Laporte was the second political murder in the history of the Canadian federation. In 1868, Thomas d'Arcy McGee, Member of Parliament, having made a brilliant speech for national unity, was shot by an Irish nationalist. Laporte, an outstanding statesman and worker for national unity, was strangled in 1970 by a Quebec nationalist.

After the assassination of Laporte, Quebec was stunned. There was a moment of hope that a united country would confront the abductors. The hope was in vain.

The new municipal party "Front d'action politique" (FRAP) had held a public assembly on 11 October, the day after Laporte's abduction. The party was preparing for the municipal elections and there was no need to mention the FLQ at all. But FRAP, too, could not resist the temptation to make political capital out of the abductions. Its President, Paul Cliche, reassured the assembly that the FLQ was not a threat to the wage-earner, that society was to blame for the violence and that FRAP aimed at taking political and economic power for the workers and therefore endorsed the aims of the FLQ. And Michel Chartrand added that he was not moved by the abduction of Pierre Laporte since "for decades the ruling classes have been butchering the workers."

After this meeting, Quebec was more divided than ever. FRAP was violently attacked by Mayor Drapeau, and the whole election campaign became extremely bitter, especially after the assassination of Pierre Laporte (17 October). FRAP was defeated.

On 14 October, the government had offered the abductors a safe conduct to Cuba if they would surrender Mr. Cross and Mr. Laporte. It would also recommend the liberation on parole of six prisoners. Otherwise, no concessions were made.

While the Montreal radicals threw oil on the fire and encouraged the FLQ fanatics to persevere, René Lévesque, on 16 October, made a last appeal to the kidnappers of Mr. Cross and Mr. Laporte, over Radio station CKAC. He said:

> If the question is still open, we ask, we literally implore, the abductors to accept the conditions dictated Thursday evening by Ottawa and transmitted by the government of Quebec.
>
> If they are still capable of thinking beyond themselves and to step beyond the awful simplifications where chaos and destruction pose as creative acts, they should at long last see that their action has brought nothing but harm to everyone, not only to the hostages and their relatives; but if they persist and others imitate them, the consequence will be a longer and more cruel ordeal for Quebec. . .

There was no answer. On the 20th, the day of Pierre Laporte's funeral, I decided to make the following appeal:

> I am speaking to you as the man who devotes much of his energies to aiding prisoners and to speeding their liberation.
>
> This is why I am constantly thinking of you and of your prisoner. We are in a deadlock and we should get out of it before Quebec is dishonoured a second time.
>
> For more than two weeks you have had time to reflect. You

have gambled. Everybody knows, and you must know, that you no longer can win.

If you love your country, I implore you to be realistic and to choose the only honourable way out: voluntary exile to Cuba and the liberation of Mr. Cross. For the sake of Quebec, do it today, day of national mourning.

Again, there was no answer.

On 26 October, Mrs. Barbara Cross made a pathetic appeal to the abductors of her husband over radio station CKLM. The appeal was broadcast a number of times, both on radio and television. It consisted of a message in English to her husband, followed by these words in French:

To those holding my husband, I express the hope that, as a victim of circumstances, he will be well treated. I beg you to free him without any more delay.

Once more, there was obstinate silence.

In the meantime, on 15 October, 1970, the Canadian government, following a demand by the Quebec government, had sent troops to guard important buildings and residences of prominent citizens. This was followed on the 16th by the proclamation of the War Measures Act — the only emergency legislation Canada possesses. (Only isolated provisions of this act were actually implemented.) These special powers allowed the government to outlaw the FLQ, until a special emergency legislation could be voted by Parliament.

On 2 November, a communiqué said that Mr. Cross was alive and well, and declared, "The established authorities have assassinated Pierre Laporte."

On 6 November, one of the alleged abductors of Laporte was arrested: Bernard Lortie, 19, ex-student. His supposed accomplices, Paul Rose, 27; Jacques Rose, 23; and Francis Simard, 23, who were hiding in the same apartment as Lortie, were not discovered, and escaped.

The Ideology of Quebec Terrorism

As we have seen, the waves of terrorism in Quebec from 1963 to November 1970 were strongly inspired by similar movements in other countries: the Maquis in France and Belgium, Castro's successful revolution, and the National Liberation Front of Algeria, which formed the first government when de Gaulle granted that country independence in 1962. Cuba is a case by itself, since it produced two revolutionary father figures: Castro and Ché Guevara. The existence of such (almost archetypal) figures is a great asset to any revolutionary movement. By projecting their own cravings onto such figures, young revolutionaries find a new identity, security and confidence. The adventurous life story of these heroes also satisfies the romantic. Youth is attracted by the mystique of the "permanent revolution" as propagated by Castro and even more by Mao, whose "cultural revolution" put the young on a pedestal and threw the "fathers" into the dust, if not into prison. For, after all, adolescence *is* "permanent revolution."

For the French Canadians who for so long had suffered from an inferiority complex, revolution means the reversal of all values, and a violent overcompensation of that complex. François Gagnon once expressed it in these words: "The fear is on the other side now." Almost overnight, social inequalities which had been taken for granted became social injustices. It became unbearable that Quebec workers should have the highest unemployment rate* and the lowest wages in all Canada. The traditional attitude of superiority assumed by the English Canadian became a scandal. The English stereotype of the French Canadian as a "hewer of wood and drawer

---

* In actual fact, the rate is even higher in the Maritime provinces, but the Quebec workers compare their lot with that of workers in Ontario.

of water" who speaks a "funny" language particularly incensed the young intellectuals who considered themselves as part of a world-wide French culture. The inroads of the Anglo-Saxons aroused the instinct of collective self-preservation of French Canada. Many pointed with horror to the state of Vermont which once had been *Verts Monts* and where the linguistic imperialism of the USA had destroyed every vestige of French culture. Even the family names were often anglicized.

No doubt the French Canadians have real grievances. They are fighting for survival. They believe that French language, culture and mentality have a place in North America. And we believe that it is not in the interest of Canada that Quebec should lose its particular French character, or that French should become a languishing language. It is a healthy sign that the French taught in Quebec is improving, and that the two thousand anglicisms which have infested Quebec French are being rooted out.

If those real grievances of the Francophones may be at the root of such extremist movements as the FLQ, and explain why they have so many secret sympathizers, do they justify the means? Having shown one side of the coin — one the English Canadians are too apt to overlook — we must also show the other side. The trouble is that bombs, riots, anti-English slogans and insults only widen the gap between the two races. They unfortunately merely seem to confirm the already rampant prejudice that French Canadians are an unreasonable, over-emotional, over-sensitive and unruly people, given to very un-English outbursts of temperament to be borne with English calm while they last.

But there is worse. Even the FLQ is not above the basic psychological laws which rule human behaviour. Whoever decides to use criminal methods to achieve political ends winds up by acquiring criminal values and criminal procedures. Moreover, one cannot long live a double life, live under a false name, dishing out lies to parents, bosses, authorities, going into hiding, without undergoing a distortion of personality. Man is by nature not only a social, but also a moral being. To preach amorality as a basic principle is to alienate oneself not only from society but also from one's brother, one's wife, one's children. This is why no real revolutionary has ever remained loyal to his wife: Stalin, so they say, did away with his first wife, Ché Guevara exchanged his wife for another when he went to Cuba, Castro has several women but no wife.

Clandestinity is a curse in itself. It gives exaggerated power to a few — a power which is bound to corrupt. In the long run, it distorts the personality by distorting the sense of responsibility and giving a wrong meaning to life — revenge. No man motivated by resentment and hate can build a new fraternal society — not even out of a sea of blood. Only those who have an answer to hate have an answer to terrorism. What we need is not more division but more understanding of how to make creative use of basic differences.

Violence only leads to more violence, revenge to counter-revenge. The vicious circle can only be broken by men who will forgive, because they know how much they need forgiveness themselves. There is no redeeming power in violence, only momentary feelings of glory at best, but there is power in loving one's brother, even if he speaks another language and is of another race.

Most of the Quebec terrorists were young people. Many of them were students who had interrupted their studies and who lived in a world of ideas rather than in reality. They had much more brain than heart, and tended to see everything in the light of their sloganized over-simplifications. Most had never worked with their hands.

All of them were extremely impatient. They all revolted against the inferiority complex which in the past had made the church-led French Canadian so submissive. The bombs were a clumsy way not only of scaring the English, but of telling the Québecois, "You can do something about it, you can take your fate in your own hands. You have more power than you think. Some of your people are ready to go to any length in order to free you from your stereotypes." This instant psychoanalysis, called *prise de conscience,* was intended to arouse in the Québecois an awareness that he had no longer to accept things as they were, and that he should not feel guilty if he broke away from his traditional pattern of lawfulness. But the means to bring about this new awareness were both puerile and dangerous. They could even be self-defeating. As time went by, they became less puerile and more criminal. Of course, the extremism of their means corresponded to the extremism of their aims: they wanted a second Cuba, or a second Algeria. On the other hand, the bombs failed to rouse the workers who obviously preferred the daily bread and butter on the table to pie in the sky.

The convicted terrorists consider themselves as political prisoners. The term implies that they are kept in prison not in punishment for any crimes but for their political opinions. Canada, contrary to France, does not recognize such a status. The League of Human Rights in July 1964 came out strongly against the concept of "political prisoners," saying that this would invite the creation of a political justice: "Political justice means policing of ideas, crimes of opinion, liquidation of adversaries. Even after the sentencing, the status of political prisoner is inseparable from the concept of political justice." The League rejected the idea that convicted terrorists should be treated differently from other prisoners.

The concept of "political prisoners" was used widely in October 1970, when the kidnappers of James Cross and Pierre Laporte demanded the liberation of twenty-three "political prisoners." It was a propaganda success to hear even the Prime Minister of Quebec, and the news commentators speak of these "political prisoners."

In fact, the fate of a real political prisoner is often much worse than that of an ordinary prison inmate. He may never be brought to court, yet he may be kept at the pleasure of the government indefinitely — that is, as long as the government considers him politically dangerous. Napoleon was a political prisoner until he died. One doubts whether our convicted terrorists would really want to share this fate.

The terrorists and their friends reject any psychological interpretations of their behaviour. They consider themselves perfectly normal people belonging to a political avant-garde. This is true, but with one restriction. A person in the orbit of an unconscious son-father conflict is not his own master. As C. G. Jung wrote, "It is perfectly possible, psychologically, that the unconscious or an archetype take complete possession of a man, determining his fate to the very last detail." Many of our revolutionaries no doubt fall into this pattern. In 1957 in his *Political Notebook*, a Quebec country lawyer named Nadeau, speaking of "autonomy" wrote, "With the crowd, this word has the effect of an incantation, of a master slogan, of some magic. . . . This is a phenomenon belonging to the pre-logic mentality of primitive society." Indeed, when one hears some young people use the words "independence," "liberation," "revolution," "justice" and "socialism," the words do become an incantation. They exert a kind of magic. When our revolutionaries speak before others of student power, black power, workers' power, one almost hears a priest invoking some divine power before an assembly of believers.

The normally abhorred concept of violence also has a particular attraction for our revolutionaries. Pierre Vallières wrote, "Violence attracts and fascinates the masses, as the ritual dances fascinate certain societies which are called 'primitive'." One terrorist wrote, "The Nation is the God, and violence his ritual."

Yet I must testify that up to October 1970, political assassination was never seriously contemplated by the FLQ, despite some pretty wild threats in *La Cognée*. Obviously, the group which killed Laporte got out of hand, probably under the influence of drugs and perversion (sadism). The curse of violence is that you never know where it may lead you.

When talking to our terrorists or when reading their literature, one is quick to discover that they are using a special vocabulary where the words have a meaning of their own. Thus the word "liberty" does not have the normal meaning of being allowed to open a shop or business, to reside where one wants, to travel abroad, to buy foreign currency, and to enjoy full liberty of expression within the limits of decency. All these liberties, which are the envy of other peoples, mean nothing to our extremists. They are "pseudo-liberties" — make-believes. Radio, TV and the press are seen as mere tools of oppression in the hands of the ruling classes. As to the liberty of trade, they maintain that this liberty is but the liberty of exploiting others. Economics is conceived as a great game played by big corporations on the back of the ordinary people.

In the revolutionary vocabulary of our terrorists every militant is a patriot, a soldier, a hero, even if he did nothing else but steal dynamite or rob banks. Anyone opposing him is a traitor, collaborator, if nothing worse. Words like "people," "democracy," or "peace," acquire an unfamiliar, even sinister meaning. And, as we have already pointed out, bosses and employers are invariably bad guys, while rebellious students and immature young people are easily praised for their "lucidity."

It took hundreds of years to obtain freedom of expression. It took a war to abolish slavery in the United States. Millions of people died that we might achieve religious tolerance, political tolerance, equality before the law, the basic personal liberties. Working hours which once were ten or more a day have been reduced to eight or less. The standard of living, during the last hundred years, has steadily risen. Most Quebec workers have a car, a growing number own their own house. Many have job security, social insurance, a pension plan, medicare. In the eyes of our revolutionaries, all this counts for nothing.

They call our society violent and repressive. Both terms are part of an ideology which was not created in Quebec. Indeed, the "liberation" of Quebec is conceived as a radical breakaway not only from the rest of Canada, but also from all the traditional French-Canadian values. Since Quebec is the only part of Canada where a Castro-like revolution appears feasible, the movement for political independence here serves as a spearhead for much more far-reaching goals.

The young feel that neither the provincial nor the federal government is capable of solving any major problem, such as the rapidly increasing pollution of air and water, the rising criminality, the shocking unemployment rate, the despairingly slow functioning of government administration. (It took eight years of bickering before the pay cheques of the Canadian government could be made bilingual! Without the measure of closure — "the guillotine," as it was called — Canada might still not have a flag of her own!) Canada needs far-reaching change, but the young have the strong impression that our governments are not imaginative enough to effect it. What dominates Canada — and Quebec — they say, are group interests to which the common good is sacrificed every time. The real decisions are not made by the government, they feel. Thus we have a general malaise which favours the emergence of political prophets of every kind.

From the example of many other countries, we know only too well what will happen in Quebec should the dreams of our revolutionaries come true. The "pseudo-liberties" will be abolished — first of all, the freedom of expression. The private industries will be nationalized and serve as a guaranty for the new national currency. The house owners will pay taxes so high (with rents fixed very low) that they will find it impossible to make any repairs and finally will only be too glad to hand their property over to the State for the amount of the tax arrears. In short, the capitalists of today will become the proletarians of tomorrow.

Any revolt against the new dictatorship would be outlawed and radically repressed. The nation will have to be adored and feared. It will possess everything, sell everything, speak and act in your name without ever asking your opinion; in short, the State will be like God, all powerful, omniscient, infallible.

A double standard is established: one for the revolutionary, and another for the rest of the population and the authorities for whom the laws are still valid. Unfortunately this double standard is already in force. During any labour conflict, the striking workers feel justified in committing criminal acts against their employer, using even bombs, and it is taken for granted that there must be no reprisal. Such a situation is eroding the law itself. Other contestants will demand the same privileges. If Canadian unions would accept responsibility for the damages caused by their members (as they do in Germany), the respect for the law would soon be re-established.

At all times, youth has been willing and even eager to invest its enthusiasm in a valid cause. In Germany, Hitler had exploited this idealism in the interest of an ideology which seemed heroic and patriotic, and which promised a new society and a new Germany. In China, Mao enlisted the same idealism for his cultural revolution. In Quebec, a number of young flock to Vallières and Gagnon.

But the bourgeois leaders had also exploited the idealism of youth.

The first world war (1914-18) was labelled "the war to end all wars" — an illusion which made millions of young soldiers march willingly to their death. After the war, a most moral principle was adopted: the self-determination of peoples. The principle changed the map of Europe for just about twenty years. Then it was overthrown by Hitler and Stalin. Hitler was vanquished, but in order to please Stalin, the principle for which millions had died in 1914-18 was never restored. World War II was fought under the slogan, "Make the world safe for democracy." It actually made the world safe for the Communist conquests. No wonder youth has become cynical.

The philosophy of the FLQ is the philosophy of class war. There is war between the workers and the employers, and there is war between the "lucid" French Canadians and the English-speaking people. There is war between Quebec and Ottawa and between the young and the authorities.

This philosophy has a very long history. It all started with the French writer Jean Jacques Rousseau who, in 1762, published a treatise entitled *Emile.* The book began with the explosive sentence: "Everything is good as it comes out of the hands of the Author of All Things; everything deteriorates in the hands of men." This was a devastating attack on society — the aristocratic society of his time, with the king on top — who were accused of nothing less than corrupting the young, the innocent, the good. And this blow came at a time when everybody felt that a big change was overdue — a "deluge" which the aristocrats hoped would only materialize after their deaths. Rousseau's *Emile,* under the cover of an educational treatise, was in fact a political manifesto which was to do a great deal to prepare the ground for the French Revolution.

Rousseau did not believe in Christianity which makes the individual responsible for his actions. Rousseau exonerates the individual and puts all the blame on the system under which the individual grows up. Man is born in a state of moral innocence and perfection, but then becomes the product of a debased environment.

The same basic ideas appear in the teaching of Karl Marx. Here, society is equated with the ruling bourgeois society, for aristocracy has lost its leading role. Man is good, but degenerates at the hands of the capitalist system. The worker is shaped by the machine he is operating, and not only the social conditions, but even the human sciences, art, and so on, are but the reflection of the system of production. The whole of Marxist teaching is based on the idea that man is basically good but that the system makes him bad. Overthrow the system and the natural goodness of man will assert itself. Rousseau's Author of All Things is replaced by History, conceived as a rational process marching towards a rational goal, and by Science guaranteeing eternal progress. The Christian concept of sinfulness and individual responsibility is rejected. (Man can do little to change the course of History.) The awareness of one's sinfulness is replaced by class consciousness. As to the fall of the capitalist system, it is seen as an apocalyptic judgement, after which a new reign will be established, a reign of such justice and harmony that governments will no longer be necessary to tell people what to do. An entirely new man will emerge.

In the Marxist system, the economic conditions govern the thinking of man. Marx believes in the primacy of matter over the spirit and rejects the spiritualistic view according to which man is free to choose between right and wrong under any economic system. Such an approach for him is only "opium for the people."

Freud's contribution is also materialistic, contrary to that of C. G. Jung. He lived at a time and in a country where adolescent acting-up was tolerated with an amused smile, but where adolescents had no real influence. Only once, in *Totem and Taboo*, did Freud deal with an adolescent culture. He explains that in primitive tribes the sons finally banded together and killed all the fathers because the fathers had monopolized the women. It is very doubtful whether such collective incidents ever happened, but this is not the point. What Freud really describes is an archetype. His legend is but a symbol of the archetypal son-father conflict. The father has all the power, he disposes of all the knowledge, all experience. If the father does not share this with his son, the latter may try to make him powerless, in order to take over everything. It is the archetype which is at work behind Quebec terrorism, behind student revolts, behind most contestations, behind the so-called generation gap. The archetypal pattern is always the same: a son who, rightly or wrongly, feels disinherited, bands together with other sons in order to strip the "fathers" of their power and their riches, if not their lives.

In this archetype, anyone who administers, provides work, exercises authority, wields economic power, is cast in the role of "father." Anyone who receives orders, has to obey, to submit, is a wage-earner, is seen as a disinherited son. The pattern applies also to the relationship between black and white in the USA, between French and English in Canada, between the natives and their foreign masters.

A revolutionary necessarily falls into the "killing the father" pattern. That the FLQ is no exception is borne out by the murder of Pierre Laporte, a model of a father and statesman, a man who spoke perfect French, a most typical French Canadian. To make such a man powerless, to make him die slowly must have given a lot of perverse satisfaction to his executors who finally strangled him with the symbol of his religious faith — the chain with the crucifix he wore around his neck.

The power of Marxism does not rest on its economic theories, some of which are no longer valid. The masses will never march for a theory anyhow. The real power of Marxism rests on the power of the "disinherited son" archetype. The genius of Karl Marx consisted in striking that inexhaustible gold mine which he called class war, and which Freud would rediscover as the Oedipus and the Totem and Taboo complexes. As the violent destruction of the atom structure liberates atomic power, division is behind the secret of "labour power," "student power." For many, the independence of Quebec means doing away with the Ottawa "fathers." Divisive ideas, hate, greed, jealousy generate enormous energy, mostly destructive. Once the goal of "taking over" or "overthrowing" is attained, this power is bound to vanish, as if by magic. This is why, after every revolution, it is so essential to continue to have an internal or external enemy to fight.

We can now understand the role of Herbert Marcuse in the context of modern contestation. This writer has modernized Marx and

Freud, addresses himself to youth and especially to the students and young intellectuals rather than to the workers. The gold mine (the source of power) is the same as in Marx: irreductible opposition against the "fathers" and their achievements.

Even Freud, the "father" of psychoanalysis, does not escape unscathed. Marcuse corrects his teaching on some important points. Freud had taught that "Kultur" (the German word means culture as well as civilization) was based on instinctual sacrifices. It was only by relinquishing the childish trait of demanding immediate satisfaction of instinctual drives that humanity achieved the more lasting cultural satisfactions. The whole of civilization, including our works of art, was based on the "sublimation" of our instincts. The energies which were denied satisfaction on the immediate, primitive level, had found a higher expression in the progress of humanity on the social, technical and artistic level.

Marcuse finds this view too austere. In our affluent society, he says, such sacrifices of instinctual drives are no longer necessary, since civilization is built up.

Marcuse's correction of Freud is, of course, in line with the wishes of modern youth. In Quebec, the same idea has been expressed by Jean-Claude Dussault in his book *Pour une civilisation du plaisir* (1968), and by C. Lagadec in the psychoanalytical review *Interprétation*. Lagadec wrote (1969, vol. 1-2): "If we only want it, the world would be but marvels. This cannot be achieved by liberating man through another form of slavery, as proposed by Marx and Freud — and all the priests — but by liberating man *from* slavery . . . from the dictatorship of reason, of memory, of ideals, of bureaucracy, of work, and of sacrifice." Truly, this is good news for the young who would like to replace hard work by *la dolce vita!*

This mentality, which considers pleasure as the highest value, is the natural outcome of an affluent society where people need less and less time for work and have more and more time to play. But it is doubtful whether any society or any civilization run by playboys can survive. Ancient Rome could not.

Marcuse calls our society "over-repressive" which means that there is still too much "obligation" and not enough "liberty." A society which imposes so many obligations is "violent." Therefore violence is justified in the fight against it. (As we have seen, this is exactly how many Quebec terrorists justified their actions.)

Marcuse does not recognize democracy as we know it. He thinks little of the great freedom our society gives to the individual. He says that the will of the majority is always bad and adds, "To work according to the rules and methods of democratic legality means to capitulate before the existing power structure." Since our democracies are based on the general will of an "administered and oppressed" population, any *real* opposition will have to be illegal.

The more Marcuse debunks the society of the "fathers," the more he flatters and glamorizes youth to which he assigns the historical task of overthrowing the present system by force. He appeals to the impatience, the restlessness and the aggressiveness of the young, and at the same time justifies their feelings of frustration and of self-pity. He projects before them the mirage of a power such as youth has never known before.

Like all revolutionaries, Marcuse is very explicit in pointing out what must disappear, but very vague when asked what to put in its place. In his latest book, *Liberation*, he at long last gives some hints as to the new society. He begins by warning the reader that it would be "absurd" to give a description of the specific institutions and workings of the new society, for "it is impossible to determine them" beforehand. The institutions will be elaborated according to an experimental method based on trial and error! This clearly means that whole nations will serve as guinea pigs to a bunch of young inexperienced politicians. Only two things can be taken for granted: the nationalization of industry and commerce and the planning of production and distribution of goods. This, Marcuse assures us, will "abolish the misery."

Marcuse completely overlooks the contradictions inherent in his system. The nationalization of the whole apparatus of production and distribution and of the exchanges with other countries would not only require an immense bureaucracy, but could only be carried out under a dictatorship. Yet Marcuse assures us that a democratic system is better than even the most enlightened of dictatorships. The free democracy he has in mind would even be a parliamentary one. The people would elect their representatives in all freedom, but they would also have the power to revoke them at any time, should they not give satisfaction. Thus, the power would really remain with the people. In order to be able to make the right decisions, the citizens would undergo a civic training and would make use of information media free of any censorship. Thus, the same citizen who might not have the right to sell a pound of apples to his neighbour, would be able to elect a parliament which might abolish nationalization! Surely Marcuse must know that nowhere in the world do we have a socialist economy which representatives of the people could question. Nor do we have a socialist economy anywhere without strict censorship of the mass media.

In his well-known book, *The One-dimensional Man,* Marcuse says that our industrialized "over-repressive" Western society creates a special type of man. Technology is seen as a form of dictatorship, since it makes man more and more dependent: "Contemporary industrial society tends to be totalitarian." Our (Americanized) society imposes a "one-dimensional pattern of thought and behaviour" which actually alienates the individual.

Marcuse deplores the loss of what he calls the "second dimension." According to him, culture used to be this other dimension, culture as opposed to social reality. Culture represented the ideals of the time. It was ahead of reality. It was not the expression of a society, but an avant-garde product. This sort of culture has gone, he says.

There is undoubtedly a lot of truth in what Marcuse writes about the lost second dimension, but many believe that it is actually religion which has always been and always will be the real second dimension, independent of the prevailing economic, political and social conditions. The Christian faith is as relevant today as it was in a feudal, pre-industrial age when economy was based on the institution of slavery. As long as man is inspired by a living relationship with God, he need not be one-dimensional. Man is neither a perfected ape nor are his convictions the mechanical product of the machines which surround him. Without doubt, one-dimensional man exists. The fanatics, the irresponsible, the playboys, the mass men have lost their depth and their conscience. They do not live; they are *being* lived and manipulated by some archetype, some passion, some complex, some mass ideal, if not by mass hysteria. Man is a free being whose decisions are only his own. Jesus Christ was free even on the cross and his apostle Paul was free in prison, despite his chains. If modern man lacks the dimension of depth, he should not blame the machine, nor the social apparatus, but the fact that he considers individual responsibility as a burden instead of a mark of nobility.

In 1968, rioting students in Rome brandished placards which said, "Marx is God, Marcuse is his prophet, and Mao is his sword." The Quebec revolutionaries would not say this. Their god is the nation, their prophets are Vallières, Gagnon, Castro, their sword were the bombs. They also disagree with Marcuse on one point: they still consider the workers as the legitimate bearers of their revolution, together with the young intellectuals. Otherwise, the approach is the same: primacy of matter over the spirit, of the stomach over the soul, of the machine over the moral values. As to the revolutionary sloganized vocabulary, this most typical expression of one-dimensionality, our Quebec revolutionaries handle it with the same virtuosity as their "brothers" elsewhere.

Two facts seem to characterize our time: (1) The small child has more difficulty now, in adjusting to reality than in the past. Too many remain "maladjusted" throughout their childhood. This is probably due to the over-stimulation provided by modern life, and to the moral confusion and permissiveness of the parents. Such children no longer know what is right or wrong. (2) Adolescence, too, has become a problem. A growing number of adolescents refuse to grow up, to take responsibility. They remain eternal adolescents. Many are eternal students. They may reach the age of 30 or 40 without ever having held a responsible job.

The most dangerous person is one who keeps the immaturity, the outlook, the rebellion, and the relative irresponsibility of an adolescent while disposing of all the powers of an adult. Hitler was so dangerous because he combined an immature, even childish mind with the full powers of a dictator.

As far as our Quebec terrorists are concerned, they belong to a very different brand than their South American and Algerian models. They are not the children of misery and abject poverty. Poverty in itself does not generate crime or violence, nor does it lead to alienation, at least not in a democratic society. Our terrorists are much rather the off-springs of an affluent, self-indulgent and permissive society. They know what they want and they want it quick — or else! They are blackmailing a society where blackmail in marriage, industrial relations, and politics, has become common-place and where almost everyone demands much more than he is ready to give.

POSTSCRIPT AT PRESS DEADLINE

4 December, 1970.

At 2:30 this morning Mr. James Cross was released. Negotiations between the kidnappers and the authorities began yesterday morning when it was finally established that Mr. Cross was being held in a house in Montreal North. The government declared that it was pre-pared to honour its previous offer to guarantee the abductors safe conduct out of the country in exchange for Mr. Cross's freedom.

The talks proceeded in the afternoon in the Canadian Pavilion at *Man and His World*, which had been declared temporary Cuban territory. An agreement was finally reached, and at 7:45 p.m. the aeroplane which had been standing by to take the kidnappers (re-portedly Jacques Lanctot, Marc Carbonneau and Pierre Séguin) and their party to Cuba took off. Upon their arrival Mr. Cross, who appears to be in good health, was turned over to the authorities by the representative of the Cuban government, and the nightmare of suspense which the country had endured for sixty days was over.

Index